70
LESSONS
Learned from my father

70
LESSONS
Learned from my father

Ryan Russell

70
LESSONS
Learned from my father

© Ryan Russell 2018

All rights reserved. Without limiting the rights under copyright reserved above, no part of this publication may be reproduced, stored in a retrieval system, or transmitted, in any form or by any means (electronic, mechanical, photocopying, recording or otherwise), without the prior written permission of the copyright owner of this book.

Published by
Lighthouse Christian Publishing
SAN 257-4330
5531 Dufferin Drive
Savage, Minnesota, 55378
United States of America

www.lighthousechristianpublishing.com

Dedicated to my dad, Roger Russell.

November 5, 2015

The lessons you have taught me over the years would fill many books of which this is just a small sample. You taught me well and if I do not display evidence of these lessons in my life, it is on my failure to learn, not yours to teach.

Foreword – by *Roger Russell (Dad)*:

After the birthday dinner, after all the gifts were given, my youngest son came back inside from having gone out to his car. He had something in his hand, a gift, I could see. His wife and kids had gathered, and I knew they were anxious to see me receive what my son had in his hand. He is a good son, academically brilliant, but not effusive in sentiment and emotion. But I did not expect what was coming.

He handed it off to me, obviously a small book in plain, clumsy, brown-paper-bag wrapping, tied with a grass string—because he knew my eccentricities, my desire for simplicity.

My kids search for unique gifts for me. I have a vast treasure of rare and one-of-a-kind gems from them—not a lot of gold value, but priceless in sentimental worth. This gift today was obviously another rare find, some written treasure, not in cost, but some small book he knew I would love, for I loved books and collected certain writers.

I have long and often instructed my kids in gifts to me, saying the words to them: "I want only a gift made by your own hand."

If there's an expensive gift to be passed between my kids and me, I want to be the giver, not the receiver. By expensive I mean…expensive to me and to them. I have never been anywhere near wealthy, and neither are they. I never wanted to be a burden to my kids.

So, I smiled graciously, and took the gift, smug with the knowledge that I already knew what it was.

"So what's this?" I fumbled. "Another gift? I thought I told you I had a one-gift limit."

"Aw, dad, go on and take it," my other son ordered.

So, I untied the grass string, remembering I had led this child to be simple and unpretentious. I carefully laid aside the string, and began to gently unwrap the small book. It was very small, not looking so old, but old in quality and binding, lovely bound, an almost light brown burlap cover, and very well made. The picture was old in tone, a simple black, spruce forest across the bottom and half way up the outer edges. I love spruce forests.

I read the title:

70

LESSONS

Learned from my father

Apropos, I thought, a clever find by my son—who was known for clever finds—on my seventieth birthday.

Then I opened the book gently. It was a new book, I could see. Where had he found it? Had he somehow gone to the elaborate trouble and expense to have a custom book printed for me? I instantly regretted the expense, knowing he was a struggling church pastor and couldn't afford it. But I never stopped smiling. There was a date page, November 5, 2015, seventy years since the day I entered the world. I gently kept turning pages.

Then I turned to the title page. And I did not comprehend.

70

LESSONS

Learned from my father

by Ryan Russell

The name was not in red, but in my eye at the time, it stood out in red.

Wait a minute…. Had my son written a book just to honor my landmark birthday, knowing my love for rare books? I turned to the next page, the dedication page, and then knew he lovingly had done just that when I read the dedication:

Dedicated to my dad, Roger Russell.

The lessons you have taught me over the years would fill many books of which this is a small sample….

And that is where the realization hit me — and I could read no further — because my eyes suddenly blurred.

This was a private book, written solely to me. But after I read as much as I could…emotion forcing me to put it down—everyone in the house read the book. And since then, a great many people have read my personal and only copy. And all have praised it.

It is my very personal book. My son wrote it and lovingly hand-bound it himself. And it is my treasure.

I wish every father had such a treasure. One of my dreams is that fathers and sons the world over have a loving relationship.

So...I would like to share my treasure with everyone, share my book...let every person, especially the loving, self-sacrificing fathers feel in some way the wonderful joy and love I have felt because of this gift.

That is my purpose with this appending of my son's book to me—adding my little part to this highly prized work, to share my book with others. Every lesson is to me and my treasure because I know the story behind it. You can't appreciate the lesson because you don't know the story behind it. For that reason I want to give that story...and make this little book of value in your eyes—as it surely is in mine.

Every father who loves his kids needs to get such a book. And you haven't--not because your kids don't care, but because they just didn't think of it. I hope they will get you a copy of this book and give it to you...and they and you will feel that wonderful love that I have felt. With this little book.

Roger Russell

LESSON 1
Kiss your wife.

The first thing you do when you get home from work. Even in front of grossed out little kids. Let them see your love, even if they giggle or gag.

****

(Dad) I didn't do this for any other reason than that she was a wonderful girl and any separation from her made me want to kiss her at next sight of her. I missed her while I was away from her. She was the source of my strength, the mother of my children, and I thought it was ok for them to see how much I loved their mother…even if they giggled and gagged.

LESSON 2
Use a long stick.

A two by four would be even better. Never use something shorter than you are tall. When it comes to killing snakes, keep your distance. This lesson has been learned well.

****

(Dad) We were loading up in the car in the driveway to go to Sunday School. My wife was in the car already, and my kids had gone around on the passenger side, the side away from the house to get in. Suddenly, coming out from the grass right at them was a big, black Cotton Mouth water moccasin—heading directly for my little kids.

I know my snakes and know the water moccasin does not fear man and will not give way or avoid a man. And they have a most venomous bite. Raised on the rivers and bayous, on a farm near the Mississippi River as I had been, I knew a couple of people killed by a moccasin bite. I ran to my kids, backed them to safety, and rushed into the garage for a suitable weapon. An eight feet long two-by-four board was the first thing I saw, and used it to advantage against the invader.

"You killed a beautiful creature," some might argue. Maybe. But if he had wanted to remain a beautiful creature, he should have never made a move on my kids.

I always wanted my kids to be wary of slithering snakes…both those who crawled on their bellies, and those who walked uprightly on two feet—and never let them get close enough to give a deadly bite.

LESSON 3
Own your mistakes.

When you are wrong, own it. Admit it and ask forgiveness. In the few times--and as I recall, very few times--that my dad was wrong or messed up, he apologized. To his kids, to his wife, to a coach on the football field. As a child watching him model this, it affected me profoundly.

My dad is my hero, and heroes don't make mistakes. But when they do and they handle it well, what a greater hero they become.

****

(Dad) A man cheated me out of something once when I was young. Or I thought he had. I blackened his name among a few people, and they shunned him out of friendship to me. He had moved away by the time I learned that I had been wrong.

The incident was closed in the minds of those whom I had swayed. I could just let it go and never be thought wrong. Instead, I took a trip and delivered an apology. Then made it known to my friends. It was a hard thing.

I always wanted to be right—to be just and fair, never wrongly accuse.

As much as I wanted to be perfect, I often was not. I was wrong—many times. But I thought the best thing a man can do is be honest with himself and admit his failures—to himself, and apologize when his failures hurt others, even if it wasn't easy to do.

It was easy to apologize to my wife and kids, because I knew they were very good people and forgave easily. It was more difficult to apologize to someone whom I already knew seldom forgave.

Forgiveness is a wonderful thing to have--for others and for oneself.

A valuable lesson I have learned is that forgiveness is frequently a greater blessing to the one granting the forgiveness.

LESSON 4
Defend your children.

Even if you have to step out of the bleachers and walk across the football field in the middle of a game to confront a coach that in anger just slung your kid around by his facemask. And this coach was a 6'9" giant.

My dad running to my defense is a great memory and a powerful lesson. And if it was another player that got slung around that you mistook for your kid, well, see lesson 3.

****

(Dad) It was my most embarrassing moment...or one of *many* "most embarrassing moments" of my life. But one I have never regretted.

It was at a grade school football game, where, from the stands across the field I saw the gigantic, six-feet-nine football coach grab my skinny little three-feet tall son by the face mask, lift him off his feet and drag him up nose to nose to scream in his face, then shake him by the face mask until his feet were flopping like a ragdoll's—all of it after some on-field error.

The next thing I knew I was in the coach's face—or as close as I could reach up to him. Ryan gave a favorable telling of my actions. What I had *actually* done was fly out of the stands, jump the six feet chain-link fence, done a four-o sprint across the field, and shouted up at the mountain of coach: "Just what do you think you're doing!!!!?" And I did all that without any kind of forethought.

Here is the sad rest of the story—the other reason I was red-faced:

It was a grade-school football game. I never thought my boy was physically suited for football, but he wanted it. So...here was the game, the first game of the year, my little son's first game ever. It was an away game, at a school I didn't know. I had left work to rush across town to find the school, not finding it immediately and arriving late and frustrated after the game had started. Much was unsure, it being the first game of the year, and I didn't yet know my little boy's jersey number. I had found him by guessing which one of the little boys out on the field was my little skinny, non-aggressive boy. I guessed: number 83. I guessed wrong. (See Lesson 3). Number 83, that the coach was shaking the life out of, was not my little boy, but a smart-mouthed kid who probably deserved at least some kind of shaking.

Truth came to me like the voice of God. But it was the half-whispered, small voice of my small son, now sitting on the bench behind the coach:
"Dad. Dad. It wasn't me."
I slumped off the field.

After the game and the anger, I apologized to the coach, even after I knew my son was not the offending and offended boy. The young coach also apologized to me. He said he had been dead wrong to lose his temper and lay hands on a student. He went on to become a great coach and great man...and never touched another one of his players.

Still, I never have regretted my thoughtless actions that day. For, with those whom I love--if it comes to a choice between cautious decorum and a sudden, thoughtless, sure, swift rush to their defense from danger—I will choose the swift defense of my loved ones every time—even if I overreact. The prime motivation was boundless love, my desperate love for my kids. I don't' mind if that is the lesson they learn.

LESSON 5
Mark Twain is America's greatest writer.

You cherished Twain, you quoted Twain and you let a boy borrow books from your library written by Twain. And now I know as well that there has never been and will likely never be a wit quite like that of Mark Twain.

****

(Dad) I take no credit other than to say I love literature and value very great men with very great talent. Twain was the greatest American writer of all time with the communicated word.

Not just my opinion. In 1935, Ernest Hemingway stated: "All modern American literature comes from one book by Mark Twain called "Huckleberry Finn." And I think all subsequent literature was influenced by Twain.

I also have an extensive collection of Hemingway, but it seems I'm the only one in the family who loved his writing. That's ok.

I collected as many of Mark Twain's words as I could find and afford. I was happy to share my treasured books of his with my kids and was gratified to see their own appreciation of such talent. And now, all of my kids can write…far better than I.

LESSON 6
Save money.

You're not going to live forever, and you certainly don't want to have to work until you die, so save money.

My father put money away for retirement and when I was older, he even asked my advice about money, like I was an expert. He modeled this lesson for me and it has become a part of me.

****

(Dad) One of Ryan's first hard work summer jobs was operating a lawn service with a neighbor boy. He borrowed my mower; the neighbor boy borrowed his dad's edger and leaf blower. They worked hard, daylight till dark, under the hot Texas sun, coming home every evening dirty and worn out, and earned every dime they got.

They were good kids, sometimes doing charity work. One day while doing one of their free lawn jobs for a widow friend, they hit a tree root with my mower and totaled the mower. They had to replace it out of their meager profits. I let them. A lesson.

In my life, earning money has been associated with hard work. That made it valuable. A great early lesson I learned was in my one and only trip to Las Vegas to visit friends who lived there. They took me to a casino.

I had traded forty dollars to a change lady for forty dollars' worth of quarters, and played the quarter slots. I finally realized I had put twenty-seven dollars into the slot machine and got nothing back. I had roofed a house for that money.

I left the casino and used the rest of my quarters to buy film for my camera. I've never been so careless with my hard-earned money since.

The future is inevitable. I knew my kids were going to run headlong into reality someday. And when that day came and they were raising young families of their own and struggling to pay the bills in their early years, I didn't want to add to that burden. No parent does. Rather, he wants to have the necessary funds to pay for his own existence till he dies, and have his funeral ready and paid for when he does die. Shoving money into a slot machine didn't seem like a good way to pay for all that.

Rather than being a financial burden to his kids in old age, a father wants to be there to throw a life line time-to-time. It can truly be a lifesaver.

I've never been wealthy, and raising kids cost a lot of money. But being a financial burden in my old age to my kids was never an acceptable thought to me. And when their time comes, I didn't want it to be acceptable to them either.

LESSON 7
Fix your car yourself.

When our cars needed maintenance or repair my dad popped the hood and went to work. I grew up believing that men fix cars themselves.
As an adult when my cars need minor work, I almost always attempt the job myself. I have almost always been successful. My dad gave me the confidence to pop the hood and go to work.

****

(Dad) Necessity was my impetus and teacher. Sometimes there was no money for mechanics. I had kids to support. I had to cut cost, and had to roll up my sleeves and raise the hood. It came with the total package of doing all a man can do to help his family, and then trust God for the rest.

Detroit taught me a lot about car repair—and how poorly they appointed access to that engine. Knuckles skinned, backs broke, sweat beaded, but the needed dollars were saved. Many of those dollars went toward buying shoes for the feet of my kids. I wanted my family to have as much as I could give them. If busted knuckles meant being able to do that, I was thrilled with busted knuckles.

LESSON 8
Pursue your dreams.

Throughout my lifetime I have watched my dad take time on Saturdays to get a notebook, a pen and a cup of coffee and write. My dad's dream is to write great books. He has spent his life pursuing that dream.
If I spend what time I can pursuing my dreams, my dreams are within my reach.
By the way, I've read his short stories, his poetry and his novels and my dad has accomplished his dream.

****

(Dad) I always wanted to write. In the beginning, I had scarce time, needing to work every paying hour I could. Still, I snatched moments here and there. I have notebooks from early years, and boxes of printed pages from later ones stuffed in every available crevice around the house.

Although none of us ever thought (fairly accurately) it would amount to much, my wife and family graciously supported my hobby, and sacrificed fellowship with me to give me that time. In the end, I find what they gave me was the greatest gift—love. They have given me far more than I ever gave them. Great kids. They must have taken after their mother.

LESSON 9
I was the greatest Tee-Ball player of all time.

Though my baseball career lasted only a short time, I have the distinct honor of being the most exceptional tee-ball player ever.
I know this because, as my biggest fan, my father made me believe it.

****

(Dad) And it was true. Ryan was a two-feet tall center fielder in one of his first tee-ball games. Out there so small in center field, he kept out a keen eye—for airplanes and birds and such. And then the other teams' last hope—their last out or winning-run hitter stepped to the plate and slammed the ball high into the outfield, right into center field where Ryan was looking elsewhere. Everyone in our stands began shouting Ryan's name. He casually looked our way, looked up, stuck his little glove straight into the air without effort or enthusiasm, and the ball fell into his glove, saving our victory.

Ryan went on to become a six-feet-seven high school varsity outstanding starter in basketball his last three years of school, a tremendous player...not by my estimation, but by the cold, calculated eyes of the coaches. But to me when he was almost too little to pick up a bat, he was the star ball player of the universe.

LESSON 10
I was the greatest basketball player ever.

Forget the NBA. During my six-year basketball career spanning junior high and high school, I achieved greatness.

My father attended all my games. He cheered the loudest and video recorded every game. These tapes became almost sacred things, not to be over-recorded with TV shows, but put on a shelf and kept for all time.

I don't recall my dad ever recording the games of Michael Jordan or other NBA greats.

****

(Dad) (See Lesson 9) Early in Ryan's high school basketball career, I once put in my two cents worth of fabulous coaching acumen where his coach had failed:
"You're a great basketball player, Ryan, but you need to be more aggressive. You'd be the best."
Ryan only smiled. "It's only a game, dad. It's for fun. When it stops being fun, I'll stop playing."
I never proffered my sage knowledge again. In spite of spurning such great advice   Ryan   went on to become a great player and pride of the school.
But Ryan eternally underestimates himself. It was a fruitless venture to praise him. But he will never know how insignificant all the hall-of- famers were, in my eyes, in comparison to my son on a basketball court, or what fabulous satisfaction I derived from watching him from the stands. My camera never missed a moment. Yes, the videos are treasures—put up and safeguarded like gold. No other valuables I own are as coveted and protected as my tapes of my kids. And never will be.

LESSON 11
Get to dinner.

Family dinner time is important. All my memories of family dinners blend into one.
My mom would cook a meal, and she was a good cook. We would all come to the table and just as we were sitting down, my dad would rush in from

working a 12-hour day. He would joke, "Y'all didn't start without me, did you?" He would quickly put his things away, join us at the table, pray for our meal and then we would eat together.

****

(Dad) I learned a lot at the family dinner table.

After the Sunday dinner (lunch to northerners) one bright, sunny, day the boys couldn't wait to get outside. Some cousins had come over and they were ready to go get to it. But we had English peas.

I loved English peas; Ryan did not. He seldom refused to eat something, but there were those little green peas. His plate was clean except for the peas. And mom had a rule: you have to try things and eat some things. His mom told him that he couldn't go play until he ate his peas.

Ryan didn't throw a fit or do anything but keep that almost smile. He did look at me, maybe in an appeal, but I was wise enough to defer to the power. He sat there as my wife began to clear the table. I got up and went to another room. When I left, the table was clear except for Ryan and his plate of green peas. When I came back, Ryan was gone, but his plate was still on the table. It was empty.

My wife smiled and said, "Look at this."

She picked up his plate, and there on the table, in a circle where the plate had been, was a ring of English peas. He had hidden them, one-by-one, under the edge of his plate. We had to laugh. He got some lecture or something from his mother, but not much else.

Going to church on Sunday morning as a family is a great thing. But for building family unity, love and togetherness, family dinner perhaps rivals it. As I ate with them every evening the good meal their good mother had cooked, I looked around the table at my kids, looking into their eyes, seeing how much they had changed from even yesterday, taking note of how things were in their worlds, for their eyes always showed it. I loved seeing how they were growing, gaining knowledge of living and becoming good people in the wide world. And looking back at me *always* was that same interest…and love.

Always keep sacred the family dinner table. It is where love is built.

LESSON 12
Go camping.

Camping is always fun. Even if the weather turns bad or you forget essentials. I can't recount the number of great memories I have of camping with my dad.
Camping in the rain and cold. Forgetting essentials like sleeping bags, cots, salt and matches (not all on the same trip). These memories are priceless.

I'm camping right now as I write this. Oh yeah, I forgot to bring salt.

70 Lessons Learned from my father

****

(Dad) Camping was a cheap (necessarily) thing my sons and I could do to spend great time together. Sometimes the whole family would go. I worked a lot of hours back then, but now and then we would catch a little time to go camping. It was always a rush to pack and head out, and often we would miss some essentials.

One cold, rainy night the boys and I showed up in the big woods and had to put up the tent in the rain. It was an old, heavy canvas tent, handed down from my dad, hard to set up, but we finally got it up and our stuff out of the truck and into the tent. Not being able to afford cots and sleeping bags as nowadays, we had as beds a sort of cowboy bedroll, a ground cover, then blankets and such. Half frozen, we got into some dry clothing and prepared to lay out our bedrolls. And then we couldn't find them. Sadly, we realized we had forgot to pack them.

Did we go home? Of course not. We slept on the cold ground and covered up with anything we could find, towels...anything. Sleeping little, shivering the night away, we toughed it out and got up the next morning, stiff, built a fire, cooked bacon and eggs and had a great day.

I was no great camper, and a worse planner, and we always got into the woods with many things we needed — left back at home. Sometimes it was very essential things: tent stakes, salt, sugar, food — even matches.

Ryan was a fun camper. But sometimes back then, he liked to test himself, I guess, and he would go into the big woods, hike way in, and camp out alone in a rough camp—sometimes for days. He still does it now and then.

But when it was all of us, we had great times, to explore and discover--and laugh a lot. We were together.

Maybe it's getting to be a recurring theme--doing things with my kids. But it was as much---no more--for my enjoyment than theirs. I loved my kids and enjoyed no one more. I wanted to lead them in whatever little things I had the time and money to afford for them.

But if I ever learned anything I have learned this: The greatest thing in the world a man can ever accomplish is to gain the love and respect of his kids. And that takes having it in bucketsful for them…first.

LESSON 13
Do what your kids love.

I've had lots of hobbies in my life. Many while a kid. It seems like no matter what new hobby I was pursuing, dad was always interested. Many times dad joined in.

Dad bought a bow when I wanted to learn to bow hunt. I never recall him going hunting without me, but every time I wanted to go, he was right there with me.

****

(Dad) We shot many arrows—straight into the heart of a hay bale. None of us ever shot anything else. But many an hour we sat up in a tree on a makeshift platform-- camouflaged, frozen, intently looking for mister deer—who never showed. We had a blast scouting out places, building tree stands, having exciting talks--dreaming.

The national forest where we could hunt for free was also mostly free of deer. But fishing with your kids is not about catching, and hunting is not about shooting into a heart so much. It is more about being in the heart of nature, roughing it, getting in touch with the ancestors, doing exciting things together. Going home empty handed was no big deal. We went home with arms-full of the greater catch—full hearts.

LESSON 14
If dad thinks it's cool, it's cool.

Little boys love what dad loves. I remember when I was collecting Hotwheels, dad once took me to the store to buy a new one. As I was busy looking at all the race cars, dad picked up an antique firetruck Hotwheel. He studied it, looked it over real good, then put it back. When it came time for me to make a selection, I picked the firetruck not the hot rods. I don't have any other cars from when I was a kid, but I still have one antique firetruck.

****

(Dad) There is one lesson I wished I had learned, learned well before I ever had kids—that kids carefully watch their parents. What we value, they value; what we like, they like; what we think is right, so do they.

If I had stopped to think of that, maybe I would have done a lot of things differently. But the truth is, I was having to learn wisdom while having a watching audience.

Now I know. We teach our children those first few very important years--not by what we say, but by what we do, how we behave ourselves, how we relate to others. I was naïve and ignorant in my own skin...but thankfully, during those dumb years I had a great father to steer me straight...my heavenly father.

I so much wish I had been that wise and faithfully-leading, and rightly-teaching parent. I'm afraid I wasn't.

But their good mother was.

LESSON 15

No cussing.

I never heard my dad cuss. I saw plenty of times when he could have. He once busted his knuckles real good while working on the car (see Lesson 7). It was the perfect time to let a four-lettered word fly, but he didn't. May my boys never hear me use any obscenity or profanity.

****

(Dad) I was a Christian...or tying to be a Christian. Jesus didn't cuss. That's proof enough for me. If I did anything well, it was because God helped me do it. Cussing is a very lousy habit at best. It is the language of disrespect. It has no place with God, and should have no place with those who work to do what pleases God.

My dad, though no saint much of his life, seldom uttered a cuss word; my mother, always a saint—never.

A man needs to have respect—respect for his wife, for his kids, for God. He needs to be able to have respect for himself when he looks in the mirror. The opposite of that is cussing—in anger, temper tantrums, selfishness...lousy behavior. I can't say I never had the lousy behavior, most regrettably. But I manage to hold my tongue.

Thank God that when my kids were listening to me and were so impressionable, *I* was listening to my heavenly Father.

LESSON 16

Fall asleep watching TV.

It must be okay to fall asleep watching TV, because dad did it. After a long day's work, when I'm sure he'd rather turn in early, he'd stay up to watch a show with the family.

I remember frequently turning to say something to my dad only to find him fast asleep.

****

(Dad) I tried to stay awake. But I was in my favorite place, and the peace and relaxation I felt of that place let exhaustion overcome me. But there, I could relax. I had no need of staying alert, of being wary or watchful. I was in a safe place, the safest place on earth…in the arms of my family.

LESSON 17

Go to your kid's games.

My dad was always at my baseball or basketball games. I'm sure there must have been a time when he wasn't able to make it, but I don't remember it. I only remember him being there and cheering loudly. I don't remember if we won or lost, but dad was there.

(see Lessons 9 and 10)

****

(Dad) There was this one game quite a ways out of town. We headed out, driving through the hectic traffic of Houston. While we were on a feeder road about to get on the busy freeway, a car came shooting out of a side street and hit us, glancing off the side of our van and then shooting on down the feeder. His bumper went flying and his fender was smashed. I knew our little van had suffered the same damage.

I gave chase, as did friends of ours, following behind us in their own car. The offending car got hung up in traffic, and we closed on him. He turned off to the right, but it was a dead end, and he turned quickly and headed back out to the feeder street where I waited. The road narrowed to one lane, and I was able to get ahead of him. My friend was behind him. We had him, I thought.

I was stopped in the middle of the one-way street. He came out behind me. There was no room for his car on either side of me because of railings. Then he gunned his car and shot through, smashing down the other side of my van and getting away.

His hood flew up and crumpled back over his windshield, and I could see that he had smashed the other side of his car. I figured mine looked about the same.

I let him go. I had my family in the van and the guy had already wrecked both sides of my van. What else would he be capable of.

We pulled in at a service station, and I went in and phoned the police. That was pre-cell phone days.

The police came, and looked over my van and shook their heads. But it was driveable and I drove it the fifty miles to the game.

We made the game. We won. We celebrated. It would take more than a couple of wrecks to make me miss one of my kid's games.

I don't know if I missed any of Ryan's games, or any of the games of my other kids. If I did miss one, it was because of conflicting schedules--two of my kids with games in different cities at the same time, and there was only one of me. I drove to anywhere they were playing, whatever town, no matter how far. I followed the yellow bus many a mile. I got there early and stayed until all the lights were out and my kids headed home. Neither rain nor sleet nor snow would stay me…and all that.

I didn't go to see them win. Win or lose I was there. I went to see them do their best, and support them doing it.

And it was not one single burden or inconvenience to me. I went to where my heart was, and it was never in some beer joint or club. My heart was with my family...and anywhere they were was the only place I wanted to be.

LESSON 18

Ask people questions.

Everybody loves my dad. You can just meet him and you like him. I was always amazed at how quickly people feel like my dad is a close friend.

One day I realized why. He has always been interested in others. He has fine-tuned the art of asking questions. He wants to know about what you do and who you are. When you talk about yourself, you become friends with the person asking the questions.

****

(Dad) Ok. It's obvious my son sees me through the forgiving eyes of love--thank God. I'm not that lovable. But I would love to be.

There is a saying—always guard your pocket book and your heart.

I am basically a quiet person, but for some reason I always spoke to the people I rubbed shoulders with in life. If I made eye contact and saw a spark of friendliness, I said hello. Next thing, I was asking them their life story.

I'm an enigma to myself. I have a dim view of the mass of humanity, but my first instinct is to like people one on one. I am interested in people, and like to know all about them. None of us are perfect, surely not me. But all of us have a story, a history. I love history, especially of people. I like other cultures, people of other places. There is something of interest in every life. And as a writer, I guess I want to know what that is.

I am a sentimentalist about my friends and always wonder where and how they fare. But life is busy and we always wander apart. That is life.

Some of us might seem unlikeable. All of us need mercy.

May I take every man as they are, knowing they have their reasons, their struggles and imperfections, just as I do—and may I also know that they are in the hands of God, as I am. Thank God it is His place--and only His place--to judge us.

LESSON 19

Gary Cooper and John Wayne are the two greatest actors of all time.

I've watched a lot of movies with my dad. And from experience and from sharing my dad's judgment, I can say Cooper and the Duke are the two best cowboys of all time. Not only that, but they are genuinely the best actors I know.

(see Lesson 14)

****

(Dad) I can see my son shares my excellent taste in actors.

I guess I like the characters they play and the characters I believe they aspire to be. A spark of character is born in most of us, but good character is built with time and great effort. Ryan must have watched my movie heroes carefully; he grew up to have great character.

But the best cowboy I have ever known was a real-life wrangler on a two-hundred-thousand-acre cattle ranch in Wyoming. The ranch was on the northern side of the Wind River Reservation, Arapaho and Shoshone country. It was rugged, wild-west desert, mountain and rocky canyon, a place suitable for the lean Indian and tough cowboy.

We were up there on a long driving tour with Yellowstone as our northernmost destination. We stopped in at the ranch for a few days to see the cowboy.

To get to the ranch compound we left the narrow, paved road, turned on to a caliche ranch road over desert and rocks that got rougher by the mile, but our SUV was four-wheel drive. After a while we turned off that wagon trail, descended down a narrow, split-rail fenced, sand drive. The road descended further and made a sharp right. We rounded a stand of cottonwood trees, and opening up in front of us was the ranch headquarters—a scattering of ranch house, foreman's house, bunkhouse, barns, corrals and many buildings of the ranch headquarters sprawled along Cottonwood Creek.

One of the cowboys welcomed us, asked our business, then showed us up to the bunk house where the cowboy we sought slept. We got out, and just then our cowboy came riding up around a big tank on a great black horse, swung down and came our way.

He was big, six-four, two-forty, that great, chiseled physique in his tight, brush-popper striped shirt--hard and lean from hard work and weather, narrow waist spreading up and into wide, thick shoulders. A horse couldn't throw him or bully him. He wore Buckaroo boots, knee—high for cactus and rattle snakes, and high-heeled for the stirrups, sweat-stained black cowboy hat, chaps and spurs. He also wore a six gun on his hip for the wolves, mountain lions and bears on the huge ranch that sprawled from the low country up and across the Continental Divide. Tucked under his gun belt were leather gloves. He also wore a big grin.

I asked the ranch owner later--a rich man who owned several ranches, farms, gold mines and business—what kind of wrangler that cowboy was.

"The best wrangler I've ever seen," he said, not smiling, not knowing me then.

The wrangler was from Texas where he had already learned about all that was to be known about tough cows and hard-headed horses.

That Wyoming wrangler and tough cowboy was Ryan's older brother, my other son, Rod. And he too had always worked hard to have good, true cowboy character.

LESSON 20

Live oaks are of the devil.

They drop leaves year-round. They mess up your foundation. They kill the grass. Sure, they look nice and they live forever, but I'd much rather look at them in your backyard than in mine.

****

(Dad) A mighty word of truth which Ryan saw firsthand.

I built the house in which I raised my kids — actually drove the nails. I also planted twenty live oak trees on the half-acre yard. That is, I planted eighteen and other ignorant squirrels planted two. I eventually cut down all but eight of them, but those eight did crack my slab and work me to death with the pruning and cleaning up after them.

Now let that be a lesson to you: keep live oak tree-planting squirrels out of your yard.

LESSON 21

Give your best stuff away to your kids.

Dad has some interesting things, but be careful about letting him know you like his stuff. If he realizes that you do, he gives it to you. I felt conflicted when he gave me his copy of an early edition Mark Twain novel. I loved having it, but I hated for him to part with something so treasured for me.

And now I find that I'm waiting for the day when I can give my stuff away to my kids.

****

(Dad) I've always loved certain things, unusual and rare, antique things, especially books of my favorite old writers. I never could afford to collect very much, but did pick up a few treasured things along.

After seventy years you begin to see the end. You realize that you never really own anything: you hold it for a while, and then it passes on.

My greatest treasure, as I have already said, is my kids. Anything I have of worth will one day be theirs anyway. It is my thrill to see them enjoy it — *see* them enjoy it now rather than not see it at all when I'm no longer here to see.

LESSON 22

Sacrifice for your kids.

When we were in the house, my brother, my sister and I always drove nicer vehicles than my dad. He once had a nice Mazda pickup truck and when I turned sixteen he gave it to me and started driving his dad's old pickup.

I love my Jeep, but I'm waiting for Matthew to turn 16 so it will be his.

(see Lesson 21)

****

(Dad) A little unexpected something extra falling into your lap now and then is always a great joy. It didn't take very much of anything to be much to me back then.

I like a nice truck or car, but status means little to me. It means far less to me than the pleasure of seeing my kids driving something they at least would not have to hang their heads over.

I have seen dads that satisfy their wants and pleasure without regard to their wife and kids. I guess I'm just not turned that way. I looked out for me when I was single, when I was my only responsibility. Things changed when I got married, and changed even more when I brought kids into the world. They didn't ask to be born. It was my decision. And it was my responsibility to provide for them until they were in a position to provide for themselves.

And even after they could and can provide for themselves, it is my pleasure to bless them with a little something extra.

LESSON 23

Cry when you spank your kids.

Mom wasn't hard-hearted, but I don't remember her ever crying when I got a spanking. "Wait till your father gets home," was never a phrase I feared hearing. Dad has always been tender-hearted. Not only did he not spank very hard, but often it would break his heart to do so. I never feared his spankings, but I hated seeing his tears.

****

(Dad) "This is going to hurt me worse than it will you."

I've heard that expression; I've lived it.

I spanked my boys three times, mostly because of quarrelling with each other. I remember them all. No, they were not beatings. I don't think it hurt their bottoms much, but it broke my heart. In that I was just like my tender-hearted mother. She hated having to reprimand a kid.

But I spanked my boys those three times. And then I sat them down and tried to justify the spankings, trying to get them to learn from it and become better people.

But the great lesson learned was by me: I would find another way instead of spankings to discipline them.

For my own good.

LESSON 24

Elvis Presley is still the king of rock and roll.

Elvis is cool. I have several of his albums. It seems like dad was quite a fan of Elvis as well.

(see Lesson 14)

****

(Dad) I *made* Elvis Presley. Well...I at least added to his wealth by purchasing everything he recorded.

Elvis hit the airwaves with "Hound Dog" when I was eleven. But long before "Hound Dog," the rumblings of the thunder of Elvis had already reverberated through my part of the world with the Louisiana Hayride, one of Elvis' first conquests.

Elvis was born and raised just down the road from where I lived. He was a local boy to us, and we would have been behind him even if he wasn't phenomenal. But phenomenal falls a bit short of what Elvis was. He still is the top overall talent package of my lifetime. He is still the standard by which all others are measured.

In my early days I played in bands and lived and breathed music. Among all the musicians I've ever known was the same philosophy: in talent Elvis Aaron Presley is the lone standout—the gold standard.

But we must be careful who we worship in front of our kids. As Ryan stated in Lesson 14, "If Dad Thinks it's cool, it's cool." I may be bowled over by singers and actors, but I give my continued support to only those among them who strive to be good people, who have respect and feelings for others. If they love God, that is the ultimate recommendation to me.

Elvis' death stuck a blow. I took the family on a pilgrimage to Graceland not too long after Elvis died. Ryan was just a boy, but he was fascinated with all he saw, especially Elvis' old pink Cadillac.

I loved Elvis in front of my kids, but I worshiped only the Great God of all creation. I am what you might call, a Jesus Freak. Jesus is all to me. I took my kids to church expressly to acquaint them with the absolutely greatest act that ever was. But in reality Jesus was no act. He was the real deal. And He will still remain Number One at the final tally. And, as the popular song out right now says: "All my hope is in Jesus."

My kids have a certain appreciation for Elvis. But they all absolutely love Jesus.

LESSON 25

Good books are worth having.

I love books. I love old books. I love reading. Some of the best books I've ever read came from my dad's library of books. Mark Twain, Charles Dickens, Zane Grey, Ernest Hemingway, Morris West.

Dad, this doesn't mean I want you to give me all your books...at least not yet.

****

(Dad) Ok. Louie L'Amour might not have been an intellectual giant. Or was he? He sold several trillion books...and though long dead, is still a top seller. Movies made from his books will be with us as long as the world stands.

At one time I had collected all of L'Amour's books...a hundred and forty or so at the time. One summer Ryan came home from college. His summer job didn't start for a few days, so he lounged on the couch and read my entire collection of L'Amour — in about a week!

I finally said, "Quit ruining your mind with books and go out and play."

He grinned.

If I had my way, every room in my house would be book shelves, and all would be full. I finally had to start downsizing. But at one time I was on the hunt for great books, especially from the masters. I browsed (drooled) in an upscale Houston bookseller store, a library of floors and glass and beauty, and every floor full of the rarest books — first editions, galley proofs, signed and sealed. And there were those almost glowing handwritten originals, and rough drafts. Prices started in the hundred-thousands.

I could only drool over those. I own some old books, but cheap ones, some I found at a musty old shop called Book Lovers, that were not so rare, but still treasures, Mark Twain being high on my list. The few great treasures I had, were gifts from my wife and kids who robbed their piggy banks a few times and bought me lovely books.

I hope those words don't inspire your sympathy. I must confess…I own the most valuable find in literature. Me alone. I own the ultimate prize, the most valuable book in existence. It is one of a kind. There is only one copy of it in existence, and I own it. Only me. You can't buy it. Money won't touch it. There is not enough money in the world to entice me. There is a lot of money in the world, but only one book of this value. Money means little; this book I own is priceless. I guard it with my life. I have let other, highly trusted people touch it, but only under my watchful and very guarding eye. It is displayed in a glass case. It must be handled with only the utmost care. White gloves would be better.

What is the title of so rare a book?

"70 Lessons learned from my father."

Now you see its great value.

LESSON 26

History isn't always right.

And neither are the ones that blindly believe it and sell it to you. History *is* written by the victors, but thanks to dad, I know that with a little discernment and research, I can get the fuller picture.

****

(Dad) How many times while watching TV or movies with my kids did I hear: "Dad! Just let us watch the movie."

I was their self-appointed censure.

Ryan brought home a book, "All the Kings Men," when he was just a kid in school. He read it, then suggested I read it. I did. I learned much.

After reading the novel, based loosely on Huey P. Long, I remembered my early learnings about the former governor.

Somehow, when I was just a kid in Louisiana, I missed the lesson on politics. But I was a country farm boy, light years away from the hallowed halls of crooked politics. I went to a little country school and if the teacher said it, it was gospel. I believed the press.

I think my education into politics began when I finally realized that everything I had been taught in school wasn't necessarily accurate. I guess I had been a doubter many times, but the realization that grown men and women would actually fake history struck me a mortal blow.

The clincher came in my realization of the differences in the accepted world view of Huey P. Long, former governor and U.S. Senator of Louisiana, and in the facts.

Long is portrayed on the world stage as a ruthless, redneck thug. The world accepts it without question. The rest of the story is that it is a made-up version of history—unencumbered with facts.

I admit—and Long admitted--that he was ruthless alright—but toward two-bit, thieving, thug politicians who had strangled the state and stolen its money. I learned that ONLY through strenuous, personal, unbiased research.

Long was raised up in the poverty of a poverty-ridden, dictatorial state. Louisiana was the poorest, least advanced state in the union. It should have been one of the richest—because of vast oil fields on its shores and along its coasts. Where had all those billions gone?

The state was owned by descendants of carpetbaggers who had taken over the defenseless state government after the Civil War and kept the power into the time of Huey P. Long. The state had few modern amenities: roads (only 331 miles of paved roads), schools, hospitals, bridges. It was a held-back, feudal state of share-croppers farming land by mule and plow, sweat and nothing more than just meager existence.

Huey put himself through law school and came out with a poor opinion of state politicians. He had learned where the state's wealth had gone—to crooked politicians who practically gave the state's vast petroleum recourses to rich oil and gas companies in exchange for personal bribes. He was determined to wrest the state away from those crooked politicians.

Long accomplished his goal, but with it came the hate of those driven away from their gravy train.

But in the four years as governor, Long created a financial revolution in the state that very quickly brought it into the twentieth century—new schools, free hospitals, all-weather highways, airports, bridges over the rivers, free text books, pencils and paper, free hot lunches...on and on—all within the four years as governor, his term was ended by term limits.

The money for his revolution was jerked out of the mouths of the rich and powerful, especially John D. Rockefeller and his Standard Oil. And Long was already a declared shoo-in to defeat Franklin D. Roosevelt in the upcoming U.S. Presidential race. How could he NOT be assassinated? He foiled countless attempts before one was finally successful.

I always wondered why the man portrayed as the worst villain by the press could be considered Louisiana's greatest hero by her common citizens. Then I knew. Nothing is mightier (and less reliable) than the power of the press.

I elected myself self-appointed guardian of my children's minds. No one else would ever be as concerned over my kids' intellectual freedom as me. But then, it was my job--the one who had brought them into the world--my duty--as essential a lesson, I thought, as how to eat.

LESSON 27

Don't overreact when a kid wrecks a car.

I expected the worst, but what I got instead was concern and mercy. I wrecked a few cars early on and when dad could have been furious, he was compassionate. I hope I never have to put this lesson into practice, but I'll be ready if I need to.

****

(Dad) Love covers a multitude of sins.

After I knew they were uninjured, inwardly I might have cringed at the financial implications: repairs, or having to buy another car, car insurance rates, all that. But such was far down the list of worries.

My kids were good kids, as responsible as young drivers can be. What they had was an accident, that second of taking their eyes off the situation, as we all have. Self-incrimination had already done its work in them. My kids knew all the details, and had already kicked themselves around the block. If they had punished themselves, they needed none from me. What they needed was understanding, compassion and forgiveness. My love and concern for them made that a simple task for me.

LESSON 28

Coffee can be drank anytime of the day.

I love coffee. I laugh at people that think it is only for the morning. Dad will put a pot of coffee on whenever he wants some, even in the evening. And now, so will I.

****

(Dad) I drink it black and strong, hundred percent Columbian preferred. Maybe it will kill me one day...when I'm ninety or so. I am blessed with good health.

I guess I'm also the product of my raising. Back on the farm coffee was the first thing put to brewing every morning.

We numerous kids had as first chores that rotated among our number, the duty first thing in the morning of crawling out of a warm bed and "putting the coffee on" — then, building a fire in the big brick fireplace if it was a winter morning. Coffee is always enhanced by cold weather. But winter or summer, making coffee was first order of the day.

It was also the end of the day. After supper, a good cup of coffee finished the meal just right.

Juan Valdez, in the mountains of Columbia can give thanks to me--I began drinking coffee further back than my first memory. I still drink it, still put the coffee on first thing, still drink it any time of the day. (I *have* cut back to six cups in the morning — shooting for age ninety-five.)

Ryan and I love to sit down to a cup of coffee when we can. We love to have a good talk — when it's just the two of us — no distractions. We both drink it black.

I never thought coffee would hurt them.

LESSON 29

Love through failure.

I hope I'll never have to do so, but since my kids are only human, I expect they will have their fair share of failure.

Because of the example of my dad I know how to love them through their failures.

(see Lesson 27)

****

(Dad) It's dumb thinking to expect anyone to live a perfect life, especially the young and learning.

I think I've said already, I love my kids. When you love, you love…forever. You don't just quit loving them because they might have failed — as all humans do.

It's because love is not based on performance. If so, God would have dumped me many years ago. He has not. Even with all my failures, He has not quit loving me. I have not quit loving my kids.

I learned that lesson from my mother.

LESSON 30

Call your mom.

I no longer have the opportunity to put this lesson into practice with my mom, but I can still practice this with others that I love.

Growing up I saw my dad take time every Sunday to call his mom in Louisiana and talk for close to an hour. And this was in the days before free long distance.

****

(Dad) In the year 1999 one of those strange panics hit world-wide. It was the Y2K scare. Y2K was the clever abbreviation of "Year Two Thousand." The world was in a panic. There was a world-wide fear that all the world's computers would shut down because their internal clocks would fail. Banks would fail. Farmers apparently wouldn't know when to plant the crops.

The panic was fever-pitch at the big company where I worked. Millions of dollars were spent trying to save the computers. I was in charge of a great many computers vital to our big chemical plant, and my bosses were on my case about "Doing something!"

I did nothing. I somehow knew nothing terrible would happen. Yet they pressed the point. I dodged the issue. Finally, my boss asked pointedly if I had prepared my computers for midnight, December 31, 1999. I said I had — that my computers were ok. It wasn't really a lie.

As I had believed, the first tick of the clock of the new year, 2000, brought not one bit of catastrophe. I felt smug that I was about the only one I knew who had not panicked — who believed that nothing monumental was going to happen in 2000.

I was dead wrong.

December 9, 2000, was one of the darkest days of my life. A few minutes before four-thirty in the afternoon my wife came home from having gone to help out a friend. She had a worried look when she came in. I asked what was wrong. She said she had not felt well that afternoon. I hugged and kissed her. I remember just how she looked, how she smelled. She always wore a perfume named Beautiful and always smelled and looked beautiful.

I remember what I said to her: "You can't be sick. You're too beautiful to be sick."

I wouldn't believe it, but she was deathly sick. She went into the den and sat down—because she knew she was sick. Yet, she seldom would go to the doctor, always downplaying any illness within herself. I asked if I could get her anything. She asked for a glass of water. I got it.

She began to tell of a problem encountered with a customer at her friend's business, the friend who had desperately needed her that day. And she told me of a belligerent customer—how that customer's outraged belligerence had stressed her, had caused her illness—her heart had a "spell."

And then she said, "Oh...here it comes again." She lay back and rested her lovely, beloved head back on the chair. She looked into my soul with those beautiful brown eyes. "I'm going," she said. Her eyes pleaded. She wanted to say a lot more. All she could do is repeat, "I'm going." Her head turned to the side on the headrest, those beautiful eyes closed, that great light went out.

The light went out of my life.

If I could only catch back those few moments....

One of the worst things you can ever see is your kids losing their tremendously-loved mother at an unfair age. I very sadly saw my kids lose one of the greatest mothers I have ever known. She was a great mom, wife—person—so loving and so well loved. She taught us all how to love. The world is colder without her.

While we had their mother, my kids stayed in touch with her just as often as they could squeeze in a visit or a phone call. My eldest son—a big football player in college—saved his quarters for the pay phone (back then) to call his mother every time he caught a minute.

My parents are also gone, but back when I had them, the old folks at home on the farm always tugged at my heart. I went far away from home, but I was never so far away physically that I was not sitting with them in front of that great fireplace, seeing their smiling faces, seeing the unquenchable love in my mother's gentle face. I so much wanted to be there in person to see it, but most of the time I could only phone.

My kids are like I was back then--too busy raising kids to come home often. But they always call me to talk. And it is the most blessed time.

Call your loved one while you have them. Tell them...tell them I, the new expert, said: "They are more priceless than fine gold."

LESSON 31

Keep stuff you'll never use.

What a treasure trove of goodness for a young boy. All the pieces of flotsam collected over a lifetime. For you it was the stuff you kept just in case you might need it one day. For me it was adventure. Crab nets, rusty tools, bits of electrical components, mysterious wonders wrapped in black plastic. Junk, most would call it. But for me it fueled my imagination when I crawled through the attic and the loft of the storage shed.

****

(Dad) And so it was. I kept everything. I might need that nut or bolt or bit of twine one day. My garage, attic, barn was full of bits of stuff. Orderly...but full.

Now, I have recently sold that home where I lived over forty years and raised my kids, and by necessity have let go many of those things kept through all their years.

Selling your kids' home is also a sad thing--if it is where they were born and raised, lived all their lives, and were thrilled to come home to. They all came back one last time before it was sold. They walked through the house, the rooms, slowly, letting all the memories flood them. It was most likely the memory of their mother in those rooms that brought the tears to their eyes. Still, it was hard.

But its ok to keep a few things. It hurts nothing. Who knows, a nineteen-fifty-model Chevy might come back and some of those parts might be needed. Or a boy might need to explore with wonder the treasure trove in your barn.

LESSON 32

Let a boy hold the light.

I know you didn't need me. At least, I know that now. But then I felt an important place sitting alongside you as you worked your wonders on some project or other. Cars, appliances, whatnot.

"Come here and hold this light for me." Magic words if ever there were any.

(see Lesson 7)

****

(Dad) I needed you…to come hold that light…to watch what I was doing…to learn…to fulfil the urge in me to show my kid some great thing. And to give me light—that great, irreplaceable light of your nearness.

LESSON 33

Organize your garage.

I can't hardly stand to let my garage get out of order. I drive by houses with garages open and chide them for their disarray. I learned from the best. The garage must be tidy.

Of course I know that organization is the only way to navigate when you never throw anything away.

(see Lesson 31)

****

(Dad) There are two pairs of expensive leather gloves stored safely somewhere in my stuff. Have been for years, in spite of many searches I have made for them the times I needed them. I found them one day while looking for something else. I said, "Good. Now I'll know where they are when I need them."
That's the last time I ever saw them.
Back on the farm there were many of us, many hands in the till—eight kids in my family, plus

a few hired hands. If anything was to ever be where it was supposed to be when needed, it had to be where it was supposed to be when not needed.

I had only three kids — or two boys (who were likely to be the culprit if any tool walked off). And I had me. I was famous for laying a tool down where I was done with it and forgetting where that was. So, we needed a bit of obsessive compulsive garage neatness. Ok...that pretty well describes me.

I hope my kids didn't learn the wrong lesson — because a man can put too much value on neatness and too little on enjoying his kids — letting them pack a few things off and not getting bent out of shape by it.

LESSON 34

Make Christmas magic.

I know you did it as much for mom as you did for the kids, but Christmas was an amazing time of year for me. With lights you put up not for the neighbors, but for us. Christmas movies. Santa Claus coming on Christmas morning.

By the way, I was a total believer the year you gave the key to the neighbor to put out our Christmas presents when we were in Louisiana.

Ryan Russell

****

(Dad) Christmas *was* magic at our house. I didn't make it magic. Kids made it magic. My wife and I had been Christmas people before kids, and after, we went a little crazy. Christmas is for kids, and we went over the top in trying to make it so. But we old folks liked a little Christmas too.

I would always take most of my vacation at Christmas, and let the fun begin. We lit up the world with lights, big tree in the den well decorated, hot chocolate, homemade wassail, cookies, pies, and goodies--gathered around the dinner table turned game table—those great board games we laughed so much over.

I can still remember the fascination of my first reading or viewing of "A Christmas Carol," or "It's a Wonderful Life." I wish I could see them again for the first time.

We had a collection of Christmas movies, and we dutifully watched them all: "A Christmas Carrol," "It's a Wonderful Life," "The Bishop's Wife," on and on. And I had all the versions, makes and remakes of all of them, as well as about every Christmas movie ever made—because I collected them, don't you know. We watched them all. We played games, we laughed, we reveled.

Then one year in December, just as we were kicking off the Christmas blowout, my wife suddenly died. Christmas died with her, and we all changed, grew up. Sadly.

But we had all those family pictures and videos of Christmases past with us together, all the memories, all the love. I regret not one light, one memory, one love.

Make Christmas memories. They never fade away.

LESSON 35

Minimize yourself.

It was never about you. Never about what show you wanted to watch or time you needed to spend away. Never about your needs first, or just putting your feet up because you deserved a break. You always put your family first.

I saw this lesson in action, but I don't know if I can ever master it the way that you do so effortlessly.

****

(Dad) No credit deserved here or needed. For I *did* do *selfishly* completely what I wanted — without a thought. And what I wanted to do more than any other thing on God's earth was be with my family, see them laugh. I enjoyed seeing my kids have fun, do well, live life happily. The payback was great. It was my great pleasure, and I greedily drank it in.

And it is a lesson I see that my kids learned well. Every one of them is just like I was in raising their own kids—lovingly putting their kids first. And just like I was—loving the reward of it.

LESSON 36

Let kids play with weapons.

People might balk at this lesson, but you let boys feel like men. We had BB guns, knives, bows and arrows, slingshots. You taught us how to shoot and not shoot ourselves. Then you let us go out into the field with these weapons. I felt like John Wayne without the horse.

****

(Dad) I have to admit—this is just a lesson from my dad to me passed on to my kids.

When I was a boy we lived on a big farm with woods all around full of rabbits, squirrels, quail, woodcock, and ponds and creeks thick in winter with ducks and geese. We always had guns in the house, and wild game on the table. The guns were almost always hunting guns, shotguns and rifles.

The same story was openly told in any farm house you went in. There would be a gun case or gun rack on the living room wall. We had just come from ancestors who had to have a gun to eat, and we still had a touch of that. Wild game was a staple to us back on the farm.

I couldn't wait for October when the first cold snap was in the air, when my dad, brothers, and I would go up to our river camp and go squirrel hunting. The camp seemed to be across the world to me then. You got there by going down and getting in a boat on Beouf River not far from our house, motored miles and miles down it in a small, incredibly slow, flat-bottomed John boat. In later months, late November, December, January, it was a freezing boat ride.

I have never been, then or since, as cold as on those boat rides. It was a two-hour ride, the boat overloaded and no more than two inches of gunnel above water. You sat still and didn't move around for fear of tipping and letting in water.

The river was full of hidden traps, logs and snags, and if you didn't know every pitfall in the black dark, as my dad did, you would shear a propeller pin and have to spend another miserable hour replacing the pin under very poor flashlight light.

But as soon as you passed the mouth of Big Creek, you knew you were past the traps and getting close, and then when you were coming up on Muddy Bayou, at its junction with the river, you would usually see a leaping fire at our camp up on the high bank where another one of our hunting party had got there early and built. The sight of that fire would warm you even if you were still a half mile away.

We had guns in the boat; they had guns up in the camp. I never knew of anyone in our camp or home, or anyone in our corner of the world being killed or wounded by one of those guns. And we had no safety drill with them. No one ever gave a gun safety course. Gun safety was inbred, built in, born in, automatic. I got the course from watching my father, as we all did.

I thought it good to pass the course on to my sons—from watching me as I watched my father—appreciating what guns could do for you, not terrified of them and avoiding them, but safely handling them—just the same way I taught my kids the automobile safety course…and that life was sacred.

LESSON 37

Eat (and drink) weird foods.

I am not afraid to try new things. You ate and drank some weird stuff in front of us and you even got us to try things we wouldn't have tried otherwise. Some of my favorite foods are mine because of your peculiar tastes.

But I don't like it all. Sorry dad, but I still can't drink buttermilk.

****

(Dad) Potted meat and cheese crackers. Potted? Sardines? Vienna sausages? The young faces screwed up.

But they weren't Vienna sausages back in the country of my youth; they were Vigh-*ee'-nee sausage*. You could order them that way in any country grocery store and get the real thing. You ordered "Vienna sausages" and you might get anything.

Buttermilk was one of the great home remedies of the old folks on the country farms. Back then we had the cows and made our own buttermilk. Buttermilk was in every refrigerator in every kitchen in the South, and not only did it enhance many a meal, it was the cure for all bowel and stomach disorders back then. And it worked.

But to my city-bred kids, buttermilk tasted like sour milk. I had a lot of fun with my kids, trying to get them to try things.

With sardines it didn't happen easily, but after many fishing trips and much hunger, they, like me the first time, ever so cautiously put that foul, fishy-smelling, guts-and-all, slimy thing in their mouths. Later, we were all great sardines eaters.

I still love the taste of sardines and saltines — but they're not allowed inside of doors. They smell up the place. They must be eaten on the river or in the woods. No compromise. And preferably—by a dad and his sons—together.

LESSON 38

Things last forever.

Okay, I know things don't really last forever, but I still feel like they should. I watched you bring appliances back from the dead and now I question why anything needs to break beyond repair ever.

I remember when I repaired an old radio (just a loose wire). When I got that thing running, I was so proud. I felt like you.

****

(Dad) My mother used to say that when I was a kid she couldn't have a clock or any such intricate mechanical thing, because I would always take it apart—to see what was inside. And it was true. I had less success putting it back together.

Don't let Ryan fool you; he's a chip off the old block. Except that he could put things back together.

I worked on everything at our house for the same reason that I worked on cars--I couldn't afford a new one or a repairman. I did get a lot better at putting things back together in my more mature years.

I still have a sixth sense of what is wrong with almost anything mechanical. For forty years I maintained very sophisticated laboratory analyzers in a chemical plant. They called me when all else and others failed. I was known as "the guru."

I wasn't the real guru. But I knew him. I called *him* when *I* failed.

He was the very best analyzer and attaching computer repairmen I ever knew in my forty years, a great, laughing guy named Larry who worked as a factory representative, installer, and repairman for Hewlett Packard analyzers. Everyone knew that Larry had mystical powers over busted analyzers. I once asked him why he was so good, where had he got such knowledge. He told me one day.

"No two analyzers have the same aches and pains. Each of 'em's got its own soul. I can't count on seeing them broke the same way twice. So...when I'm driving down your plant road to come repair your analyzer, I call on the great repairman in the sky. I ask God to show me how to fix it," he said with a smile.

I understood. I also got my knowledge from the same source.

And that same source can make your things last forever...if you need them to.

LESSON 39

Build your house.

I'm not great at this, but I know I need to try. You built our house, literally, and you fixed it whenever it needed it. You are the gold standard of taking care of a home. And not just the foundation, walls and roof- you built those within into a family.

****

(Dad) Sorry, Ryan. I need to correct you on this one.

Yes, I built the physical house (with the help of a master carpenter father-in-law). It took some months, and my boys were there a lot of the time, running all over, getting into everything, excited by it all. It also took a lot of hard work. We built it well—solid and right. But that was just the outside of it.

The inside of the home, the strong part—the strong family, the good happy, loving home was not built by my hand. That part, the great heart of our home, came under the gentle hand of your mother. I think if you'll think about it—you too will see that this lesson came from her.

LESSON 40

Write letters.

All of my adult life, you have written me letters. Sometimes with a check enclosed to help me out. Sometimes on my birthday. Sometimes just to put into words what you wanted to say. A phone call would have been easier, but you took time with pen and paper.

I've kept those letters.

****

(Dad) Well…yes I did write letters to my kids. They were love letters.
    And I have every letter my kids ever wrote to me. They are *loved* letters, carefully preserved.

LESSON 41

Show your kids who they are.

In those letters (see Lesson 40) and in your poetry, you've displayed my life as seen through your eyes. As no one can see themselves accurately, you've given me a tool to see myself more fully. Those written words don't change who I am, but it has changed how I see myself.

****

(Dad) I wonder who taught who.
  Please let me insert an example, an apt poem I wrote twenty years ago about life with Ryan.

GIANT

He came along two months early.
Couldn't wait, it seems, to get started.
Littlest thing I'd ever seen,
But even then, big-hearted.

Didn't weigh five pounds.
Wasn't much over a foot and a half long.
I could hold him almost in a single palm.
Even then my heart was long gone.

He took it soon away--
Forever--with that happy little smile.
From the beginning a sweet little thing,
Contented, a heart-thieving child.

Having rushed his arrival, there were many problems,

70 Lessons Learned from my father

But complaining was never one of them.
Even sick and sometimes hurting
You seldom heard a whimper out of him.

I laughed many a day to watch him play.
He could play with a dozen or alone.
The smile was still the same,
In a crowd or on his own.

How could you not love such a sweet, pleasant, little child —
Even till this very day.
Alright. I'll go ahead and be honest:
I never thought to try and find a way.

Such a little child--he was his two-years-older brother's doll.
Dressed him up in every kind of old hat and clothes.
Played with him each and every waking moment.
Loved him like us all, heaven knows.

You may think, from the way I think, that I think he's perfect,
But I guess I know he's not.
But who is or ever was except Jesus Christ.
But this child of mine was good and kind, and I sure like him a lot.

He never was big as a minute
All those years and happy days,
But I've never seen a bigger heart.
It was a giant's heart in all its ways.

How many lessons that child taught *me* his growing years.
Taught me, with that giant's heart, to see the good.
Taught me to overlook outside and look inside
As I now know I should.

He wasn't the most popular child to ever live.
He wasn't loud or always so big to catch the eye.
But of those who took the time to look,
They saw that giant's heart as big as the sweeping sky.

Quietly he went his way, did his thing,
Always with that happy smile on small face.
While others whirled around him, madly
Eager to finish first in any race.

It was his serenity that amazed me.
There seemed to be only one he thought to please,
Himself--live the standard he had set.
But he did that with ease.

Not that the standard was low.
It was incredibly high to see.
He had a set of almost unreachable rules
No thanks to me.

It was the rules of a giant's heart.
Not attainable by smaller men.
It said be honorable, do the right thing,
Be kind and good until the end.

And the child lived it.

For that reason, was comfortable with his life and part.
He had done his best to be his best,
Had done it with his giant's heart.

Pee wee baseball -- he wasn't much bigger than the bat,
But he stepped up to the plate and swung it all the same.
Laughed when he hit; laughed when he didn't,
Said, don't fret, Dad. It's only a game.

Tried out for football like all the rest
Did well, but knew he was too small.
So, with that same, secure smile, turned to another game,
This time it was basketball.

Yes — he was too small, but had him a coach that was a better man than me.
Taught them how to win, but more importantly, how to lose,
Because losing always goes with winning,
But to go out mean or in dignity is ours to choose.

Coach told them eloquently by no speech but huddled, pre-game prayer
That the meaning of the game and life ran deeper,
Because in the game, and especially the rest of life,
There is another watcher and just scorekeeper.

Something happened one summer. My little child grew.

We look around and that little, little child is growing to the roof
Six-foot-seven on the basketball floor, towering over all
Living, breathing proof…

That sometimes we do grow, grow to fit our heart.
That's why some of us stay small and tiny and mean, cunning and smart.
And some of us, like my little child, grow tall and good
A gentle giant, with a great and good giant's heart.

Roger G. Russell
March 10, 1997

LESSON 42

Show your kids who they can be.

You believe in me. In those written words (Lessons 40, 41) sometimes I know you've gotten it wrong. I am not as good as you have made me out to be, but I forgive your error due to parental bias.

But this too changes me as now I aspire to become the person you describe with your words.

****

70 Lessons Learned from my father

(Dad) You watch your child grow up and spread his wings as would a father bird watching his fledgling swaying on the tree branch finally about to jump and launch out into that unknown world. It might be scary to the bird parent, but to the human parent it is a great mixture of terror and vast pride. Sometimes the baby bird doesn't fare so well on the first attempt, but is hardier than perceived. And the lesson is learned well, and next time he does a better job. So do human kids.

Ryan launched out of high school near the top of his class with high honors (he said he didn't want to be valedictorian because it came with fanfare). He had a scholarship in engineering at The University of Texas and perhaps too much confidence. He made some mistakes, he took the bruises, but on his next time out, with some teaching bruises under his belt, he did everything right. His second landing was far better.

Today, he holds a very worthwhile position and the esteem of a very many people.

We can learn good lessons from the bird parents. The parent birds don't fly off and abandon their fledgling because he made a rough landing the first time out. They huddled over their baby. They will be there to charge anything that draws close to that baby on the ground. And so does the loving human parent.

Ryan has reached higher heights than I could ever accomplish, with a very responsible position where many follow him with confidence.

I take no credit, again bowing to his wise mother. I kept him fed; she kept him steady in the boat. But I always totally believed in him and could clearly see the potential he had in him.

And I wanted *him* to see it.

LESSON 43

Build contraptions to help your kids.

Part of the reason that I was the best tee-ball player of all time was because you made a homemade tee for me to practice with at home. And who can forget the baseball on a rope you swung for hours to help us learn to hit.

(see Lesson 9)

****

(Dad) I've never forgotten the rope on a string; neither have my sons.

I loved helping my boys learn a sport. Well...most of it. After they got into live arm pitching, and my boy was a pitcher, there was one time....

I played catcher, giving him pitching practice. Once there had been drenching rains for days, and the back yard was a bog. We had this long driveway, so brilliant me decided we'd take the practice to the concrete.

If you don't know, listen up. You can't play catcher on concrete as safely as on dirt. Some balls hit low and turn into rocket-propelled grenades seeking out soft targets. And you can't fall on your knees to dig them out or dodge them.

One very well thrown fast ball hit the concrete where the bag would have been and turned into one of those deadly missiles. But I caught it alright…right in the crotch, and as they say…the rest is history. My last practice on concrete.

The rope on a string was a good idea for a tiny budget. And I don't think I know of any such contraption for any price that works better. They have these nice, clever, one-man hitting contraptions now that are pretty good. They eliminate the need for dad to be there. Now he can be off on the golf course enjoying his buddies.

The rope on a string involved drilling a hole through a new baseball, running a string through it and tying a knot on the end so it will not pull back through. It also involved a patient dad on the other end of the string.

It sure wasn't wasted time. If it gained nothing else, it gained in truckloads an unbreakable bond between father and sons. I wanted them to know I was there for them, would go to any lengths and build any tower from which they could launch.

I still am. And I think they learned that one well. I see them passing it on to their kids.

LESSON 44

Let a boy take things apart.

How many household items did I destroy, just to see how it worked? You could have said, "stop making messes," or "stop breaking things," but you let me explore through disassembly. I broke things, I cluttered your garage because I wanted to be able to put things back together like you did. And you let me.

(see Lessons 33, 38)

****

(Dad) As I commented in another lesson, Ryan as a boy was a copy of me as a boy, because we took things apart...and my parents let me live. But every now and then I was able to put it back together. Ryan *really was* better than I had been at reassembling a working item.

You can't fault a son for having your faults. His faults *is* your fault (poor grammar intended).

Your best first tool for dealing with a boy like this is love. Your second-best tool is patience. I had enough of the first to overcome the lack of the second. So did my parents.

Stock up on love when you have a son. But that comes mighty easy.

LESSON 45

Give kids chores.

We had a big yard, and when Rodney and I were old enough, it became our responsibility to keep it mown. I hated grass cutting day. I hated the work and the sweat and the time I lost playing. But most of all I hated the times when we procrastinated and you went out and did it yourself. I hated to fail in my responsibilities. You taught me that with a lawnmower.

****

(Dad) I was no great fan of work back in my youth either. I was raised in the work era in the work capitol--a pre-mechanized cotton farm, a big one in Northeast Louisiana, not far from the great river, the Mississippi. It was an ocean of work— large corn fields, hay fields, twenty-acre pea and bean field, five-acre vegetable garden, five-acre melon patches, ten-acre fruit orchard, pecan orchard, blackberry vines, mayhaws, persimmons. There were a hundred and fifty cows, ten of them dairy cows that needed milking early mornings and late evenings, fifty work mules, varying herd of horses, from forty to eighty hogs, a mess of goats, a sea of chickens, ducks, geese, and even a big flock of guinea fowl.

Work. But the thing that took more work—more, hot, back-breaking work than all the rest combined, was our thousand acres or more of cotton, the money crop. Cotton, as we raised it when I was a boy, was all done by mule and by hand.

Disks, plows, planters, cultivators were all mule-drawn. The rest was also done by mules—like me.

I chopped a million miles of cotton then had to go back and hoe it. What?

There is confusion amongst the unenlightened about the subject--northerners, writers, or news people who refer to all hoeing of cotton as "chopping" cotton. Not true. There is chopping, and there is hoeing.

Chopping predated hill-drop planters which planted a "hill" of three plants every eight inches. The old planters sowed a stream of seeds and the plants sprouted that way--an endless stream of plants about a half inch apart—down the long row that ran off into the heat-shimmering distance forever.

The stream of plants had to be thinned out--chopped. The grass wasn't worried with on the chopping pass through the fields. The next frolic pass through the field would be for the grass, to "hoe" it out from among the cotton plants so the cotton only would flourish.

A qualified cotton chopper could "chop" cotton at speed, almost in a casual walking pace — steadily bringing down the hoe repeatedly as he walked and leaving those three stalks every eight inches. (I use the gender, he, as a writing contrivance. Ladies, don't be fooled. My poor sisters were right alongside me, chopping away under the hot sun.)

Chopping is a learned technique. What the unlearned, non-chop-qualified little idiot will leave behind him is a butchered mess. He has to learn — the hard way — by mortal fear of his father's fifty-inch belt. But it is an amazingly quick teaching tool.

Thank God my kids didn't have to raise cotton — although, in retrospect, it is not so bad a way to be raised. However, I wanted my boys to know there was more to life than watching cartoons and video games in cool air conditioning. They learned to do physical work and sweat. They also held paying summer jobs all through their high school days, and never complained. They were good boys — as was my daughter who came later.

My two boys were opposites in one thing: one was ok indoors, one was not. You couldn't punish them equally by sending them to their TV-free rooms. We punished one by sending him to his room, the other by sending him outside.

We gave them chores to prepare them for what was to come. For the boys the chores were more outside than inside. But "outside" in their day was a far country from the hand-worked cotton field of my day.

That was real chores.

LESSON 46

Polish your shoes.

I learned that men polish their shoes. All things including shoes last longer when you take care of them. I watched you take your shoes and your polishing kit out of your closet and go to work.

It sounds stupid, but I felt a great deal of pride when I bought my first polishing kit.

(see Lesson 38)

****

(Dad) Ironically, I was reading a business magazine a few months ago, and there was a picture of a man polishing his shoes. The ad was to personnel directors and said, "Trying to choose between two good job applicants? Choose the one with the polished shoes. He will also take pride in his work."

All my kids take care of their appearances. They are clean, well-groomed, and well-dressed.

Not one of them has a tattoo or body piercing. I don't know if it helped that I told my boys that if they showed up with an earring, I would surgically remove it—without anesthesia.

When my eldest son, always a prankster, was a senior in high school, he came to our house one evening with all the football team's defensive line, of which he was a part. They were fearsome that year, blowing through offensive lines, not losing a game. My son had far outgrown me by then, and some of the boys coming in with him were upwards of six-five and two hundred and seventy-five pounds—all of it muscle and twice as big as me. My son was to the rear, coming in last, and leading him was a pretty fearsome foursome, but they were all grinning. I smiled with them sensing by the type of grin that something was up.

And so it was. The defensive line parted, and there was my son. He was grinning, head turned to one side, then he turned the other way—and there, hanging from his ear was an earring.

I stopped grinning, stood up immediately, and started for him. Seeing my look, the big defensive tackles half guarding him, quit grinning and gave way. One of them later said to my son, "Your dad scared me."

My son turned serious too. He quickly jerked the fake, magnetic earring out and said, "Dad, it's fake. It was a joke."

I laughed about it then, but I think my son and all his huge buddies learned something of my narrow-minded opinion of men's required attire. To this day neither of my sons, nor any of that big defensive football team—who are all my friends-- have ever worn earrings. They have all become successful, and good, still-smiling people, neat in appearance.

And they all shine their shoes.

LESSON 47

Go home.

We took many trips to Louisiana when I was growing up. You went to see your family, but through you it always felt like going home. I never lived in Louisiana, but a big part of me feels that those fields, forests and rivers are my home too.

****

(Dad) My kids roamed those fields and forests--swam, boated and fished the rivers.

We all perked up when we had the van packed and were headed to the old home place in Louisiana, especially at Thanksgiving and Christmas. We had some great trips, but a bit long for restless little boys. They didn't have video players, Gameboys, cell phones and the plethora of mind-numbing devices kids have today.

But we had a ball playing the many games of the road, our favorite being to go through the alphabet, the winner getting through the alphabet first by spotting, on road signs, words that began with the next letter. We also divided up and counted cows on our sides of the car. You counted as many cows as you could as you passed. A white horse let you double your score; a cemetery and you lost all your cows.

One thing I always had was the longing to go home. More than blood flows through our veins. Loyalty, belonging, family, the hills of home are there too. Southern farm families are close and cherish and guard their family ties. My kids were raised in the city—but the old farm flows to them through me. They too long for home.

They came home, always—drawn by the unbreakable bonds of family love. And when they showed up at our door, coming home from college, or with their families after they married, I was ecstatic. We all were.

Go home. I hope the love is there as it was for me. If not, work to make it so. It is one of life's greatest blessings.

Ryan Russell

LESSON 48

Tell stories of your family.

I never met John Russell. He died long before I was born, but I feel like I know him, at least some part of him. He doesn't feel like a stranger to me, but somehow a part of me. You told me stories of him and many others. You gave me a sense of who I am by introducing me to those from whom I came.

****

(Dad) John Russell was born in 1893. One night in about 1920 John Russell went to war — a private war. He declared it when his younger brother's horse came racing panicked into the yard. A rope was tied to its saddle horn, and back on the end of the rope was John's brother, tied by the ankles — dead, badly beaten and then smashed to pulp because of being dragged home through the woods at a full gallop — two miles.

John Russell knew where the horse had run home from. A couple of miles through those thick woods, down on the river, was a big family, a family who had a grudge against John's brother because he liked one of their girls.

That river family had multiplied to a few houses, a settlement on the river. John Russell saddled his big black stallion and headed there. In his holster was a Long Colt; under his belt were two more.

He rode up into that compound of houses and called the men out.

They came out with pistols and squirrel guns to face one man. He called down the wrath of God on them, he the death angel. When the guns fell silent
and the smoke cleared, men lay littered around the place. Some were dead. Some had fled into the woods.

John Russell was still standing. He was shot a few times but standing. He climbed back on his black horse and rode out to the sheriff.

I didn't know that story for my first years and wondered why the remnants of that family stepped respectfully out of my way as if I were a grown man, even when I was just a kid. I thought they were just shy. My all-wise, mischievous older cousin one day finally told me why: John Russell.

Back down toward the roots of our family tree were some real characters, strong men who tamed a wilderness. One of them is Ryan's great grandfather who cleared a farm in the Choctaw wilderness. He also fought the stigma (back then) of being half Choctaw Indian. Fought it well.

But his eldest son, John Russell, still stands out.

I knew Uncle John from my earliest memory until I was a young man. And I can still remember the sight of him sitting tall and straight on some big black stallion. He preferred stallions, and black ones--big. He was tall and had huge hands. Men stepped out of his way. But the strange thing—he was a pleasant, smiling man.

Our world back then was a farming community, all of us living within a circle about ten miles wide. Right in the center of that circle was a crossroads. On one corner was the sprawling, silver cotton gin, and across on the other corner was John Russell's big general store. He built the store in his later years after he retired from farming. I can see him now behind that counter, welcoming customers, big and smiling. I couldn't pay for a soda water in that store.

Thinking back on his life, the one thing that impressed me most back then and defines him to me now is the way he celebrated Christmas. On every Christmas day you could expect a visit from him. There were thirteen kids in his family, eleven of which reached adulthood and had several kids—a large family. Yet, at some time on the day of Christmas you would see tall John Russell ride up on his long-legged black stallion horse, step down, and laugh as we kids swarmed him. For we knew why he had come.

Sometime before Christmas John Russell would go all the way to town, to the bank, and take out a bag of new silver dollars—real silver. And when he showed up at a relative's home he had a pocket full of them. One-by-one, beginning at the oldest child, he would dig into his pocket, come out with a silver dollar and hand it to us. It always came with one, long, hard hand on one of our shoulders, the other to rub our heads. And that smile on his face was of pure pleasure.

As Dickens said, he was a man who knew how to keep Christmas. He taught me how—and now, though long dead, he is a worthy teacher of my kids, and one I am grateful to have as my family.

Ryan can take pride in the old folks back in his past, most of them. For back then, honor was the most sought-after trait. Without it, a man felt naked.

Those are the good stories.

LESSON 49

I know what a "Pawpaw" looks like.

I don't know how much longer it will be before I have grandkids of my own. But I have a good template of what a grandpa looks like and what he does. I want to be a grandpa to mine like you are to yours.

****

(Dad) I love my grandkids because I so loved their parents. My kids weren't perfect as I am not perfect, but looking over the broad spectrum of kids that were contemporaries of my kids, I think mine graded out well by world opinion (top of their class by mine). Not that they turned out fantastically financially successful and stood the business world on its ear. But they did become the salt of the earth, good, kind, generous, forgiving, hard-working, honorable people of whom no father could be prouder.

And they have fathered and mothered kids just like them—my grandkids. I've heard the joke—if I had known how wonderful grandkids would be, I would have skipped the kids and just had grandkids. Funny. But totally false with me.

If I have ever terribly overdone the love for my kids--have just plain stupidly, blindly, gaggingly been absolutely too crazy about my kids--I do not beg forgiveness. For that is just what I set out to do, and ended up justified in doing it. They have been kids worthy of a father's love.

And their kids, so much like them, are also so easy to love. I hope you are as blessed a father as I am. Grandkids are fabulous. But there is something irreplaceable about your very own kids. Grandkids are just an added addition to that love. A lesson I have absolutely learned.

LESSON 50

Kids never grow up.

Well, sure they do, but they never stop being your kids. You've told me that time and time again. It was like a repeated mantra and now that my kids are growing older I feel the truth of those words that I learned from you.

And I will always be happily and gratefully your boy.

****

(Dad) (See Lesson 49) Ryan was always a smiler. Whether playing alone or with his brother, or others, he had that big smile. I thought I could never love anyone as much as my first son. I was wrong. My second son immediately carved out his place in my heart. And when I saw that smile I just wanted to grab him and hug him and kiss him. He wasn't much on all that affection, but I couldn't resist it.

And if you think I don't still feel that way about him, then you would be wrong.

I know now that same feeling lasted a lifetime in the great heart of my mother. The expression she cast on me the day that she was dying was that exact same expression I had seen on her kind face all my life, back to when I was a little boy when she would snag me, as I had to do Ryan, and would squeeze me tight in a hug before releasing me back into the wild.

You never change—I don't—haven't, about how I love my kids. I guess, like my mother, I will only change when my eyes close their last. But the very last look I cast on my kids will be like the ones I cast on them now—total love.

You will always be my child.
LESSON 51

Take family vacations.

Some of the greatest memories of my childhood are the vacations we would take as a family. Whether it was at the beach, taking a road trip to Graceland or camping out at Petit Jean Park, I cherish those memories. I hope you can now laugh at the time you thought I fell from a cliff and died.

(see Lesson 24)

****

(Dad) Ryan was about nine when we finally went to Memphis to tour Graceland.

We started out from home in Houston on a road trip, and Graceland was our ultimate destination. But we would go by way of the Ozarks, Eureka Springs, through Branson, Missouri, then follow the beautiful White River southeast toward Memphis. The vacations I remember and loved best were like that—gathering all my kids together in a small place, being with them, showing them the world.

Petit Jean was a favorite, a beautiful state park in a string of beautiful state parks in Arkansas, most of which were built by the WPA (Works Project Administration), a government program during the Great Depression that gave men a chance to earn money to feed their families. In those days a man wanted to earn his money. These days they are content to lie on the couch and just get the government check in the mail. But that was a different caliber of men; they wanted to earn their bread.

It was at Petit Jean that Ryan scared the life out of me. It's a rugged place with the largest waterfall in the South. The waterfall emptied into a great canyon that the river and falls had carved out in some great ancient flood. You can hike up along the river in the bottom of the canyon to see the falls, as we did.

My nephew and his family had met us there, and we all made the hike together. On the way back from seeing the beautiful falls I saw the ever-curious Ryan headed up the steep wall to the top. I yelled at him to come down, and then got absorbed in our crowd, dumbly thinking my son would heed my warning. In another minute I checked to make sure he had complied. He was gone.

In panic I went looking. I climbed up to the high rim and onto it, scanning the terrain. No Ryan. A trail traced the rim, and I made the decision to take it to the left, trying to put myself into my son's mind. The left was obvious: that way the canyon opened up most scarily. The walls became straight, sheer drops four hundred feet to the rocks below.

I practically ran, going to the edge now and then to see if my fearless son might be lying down there on the rocks. At one place the wall and trail made a sharp bend creating a point, and just off that point a spire came up parallel with the wall, ending in a flat--topped circle about a dozen feet wide. Between the point and the flat top of the spire was a distance of about six or eight feet. Still in Ryan's mind, I could imagine him being unable to stop himself from trying to jump from the edge to the spire. In great apprehension I cautiously crept to the edge and looked down. No Ryan lying broken down there, thank God.

A young couple came into sight around the bend. I asked them if they had seen a kid, a totally dumb and fearless (and in major trouble) kid up the trail. Yes, they had seen him. He had been flying up the trail, away from me.

I broke into a run in that direction. I had gone a good distance when that kid of mine broke into the open around the bend, running back toward me. He knew he was in trouble.

He really knew it when he saw the look on my face.

"You are in big trouble, mister," I said fiercely.

But when he hustled on up to me, I hugged him. My son that was dead was alive again.

I renewed my already well-known but temporary rule that Ryan had to be constantly watched.

The last pleasure trip we took with Ryan, together as a family, was when he was still single and a student at the University of Texas. That summer we hopped in my four-wheel-drive SUV and headed up to see Ryan's brother, the wrangler on the vast cattle ranch in Wyoming. It was a two-week trip, but a wonderful one. We stopped at any interesting place we came to.

Ryan did all the driving, my nearly grown daughter sitting up front in the other seat. My wife and I relaxed and cuddled in the back seat, often laughing at our two kids up front.

We spent some time with the cowboy, then he followed us on up to Cody and Yellowstone, and after Jackson Hole, we had a tearful parting as he headed back to the ranch and we went south. We took several more days getting home, following the trail of the Anasazi down through Utah, Colorado and New Mexico, going to the bottom of the U. S. at the Rio Grande and Judge Roy Bean's Law West of the Pecos at Langtry before turning finally toward Austin.

We did take one other family trip after that, but there was no pleasure in it. It was a Christmas trip, back to Louisiana, this one with the addition of a daughter-in-law, my eldest son's wife. But to offset the addition of the daughter-in-law, one of us was not. We were absent the whole heart of our family; my beautiful wife had just suddenly died a few days earlier—and those of us remaining, not knowing our next step, decided to go home for Christmas the last time.

We huddled together as for warmth, but I was thankful for every memory, and thankful we could cling together now because we had learned how to draw strength from each other by clinging together during all those wonderful trips—when it was a time of laughing.

Ryan loved to explore. But if you went out with him, better lace up your hiking boots real tight and hold on.

But how so very much I loved those wonderful times and trips with him and my family out in God's great creation. It binds forever.

Family trips with loved ones. Take them while you can.

LESSON 52

Be the prodigal's father.

That particular story from the Bible has great significance for me, because I lived like that lost son for many years. And through it all you perfectly displayed to me the heart of that father in our own real life parable.

May my kids never experience that, but if they do, I know how to be their father through it, because of you.

****

(Dad) Ryan was never a bad kid, but he was a human kid, and all human boys follow the built-in pattern as they grow. They have to eventually try their wings. I understand; I was a human boy.

You wish they would not make the mistakes you made, but usually, that is impossible--and always, it is a foolish expectation.

When the Prodigal Son failed, his father did not condemn and disown him. Instead—he watched longingly and lovingly down that dusty road. My parents didn't condemn or disown me. I didn't—I couldn't have disowned my kids.

Why? That's a simple answer: love. I loved them. Fathers should love their sons without qualifications. We should love them so much that it becomes a "no-matter-what" love. Most fathers have that. And we parents should never expect our kids to be wise, perfect saints. They can't; they came from us.

I was sometimes disappointed that my kids made mistakes, bad choices, that they didn't think with wisdom of seventy years when they had only seventeen or eighteen years of experience.

God has a sense of humor. He made us that way. Maybe we are supposed to pay for the problems we caused our parents by having to deal with those same problems from our kids. Or maybe He knew we learn best from experience.

The kids who never make wrong choices are those who are not given the liberty to make their own choices. Whereas this might be good policy when it comes to concrete tangibles such as money and things, it usually doesn't work with blood and bone and feelings and emotions. For a parent to try to suppress that in a child is to invite a future of an explosion of pent up frustrations that may be irrecoverable.

But there was not much philosophy in the Prodigal's father as there was not much philosophy in me. He loved his kids as I love mine. And when mine were away from me I have always looked down that dusty road with the hope of seeing them coming.

And when I did finally see them coming, my heart thrilled.

I wanted to kill the fatted calf. Celebrate.

Simple.

LESSON 53

Make up words.

How many words did I use growing up thinking they were real words only to find out later you made them up. I now love making up words for my kids, just like you did with us.

****

(Dad) Ryan was a great speller. There was a teacher who pressured him to compete in spelling bees contrary to his own proclivities. He did well. In one spelling bee he was steadily eliminating competition when he was presented with what might have sounded like a simple word. But it was one of those that has no phonetic spelling or real reason to exist. I knew it well but couldn't begin to spell it. The crowd around me groaned, and I knew they felt like me—who can spell it. You just had to memorize the spelling.

Even at that, Ryan almost spelled it, putting only one logical letter in place of the actual nonsensical one.

But I doubt he could ever spell my made-up words. I was bad about making up words. I realize I should have made it clear that the made-up word was a dad-word and that dad was weird. And saying a dad-word in public might gain a skeptical look.

I'm a lover of words and can't help tinkering with the English language. But it was unfair to my poor kid to spit out a ridiculous word learned from dad, thinking it Webster-proof in front of his young peers whose sole purpose in life was to find something to laugh at in others.

My kids all have a great sense of humor and fun. Maybe it was the dad-words.

But in spite of the dad-words, Ryan was an honor society student who never seemed to crack a book but aced every exam and won scholarships. All my kids did well in school — in spite of dad-words.

I repeat: they had a very sharp mother.

LESSON 54

Always know exactly how much longer.

On all our road trips, like kids everywhere, we asked, "how much longer?" You could not only tell us exactly how much longer, but how many more hills, bridges and curves were left in the road.

I too now know exactly how much longer for my kids, but not as well as you. They then turn to Krystal and ask, "how much longer really?"

(see Lessons 47, 51)

****

(Dad) I was born and raised in that country we traveled so often—all those trips to my old home. I loved it; I knew it's every twist, turn, landmark, spirit. On the drive--after we got into Louisiana, I was Google Earth. I had made that trip all my life, thousands more times than the Google Earth car. I knew it's rivers, bridges, roads and potholes. I knew what was coming up, not only around the turn, but in my mind, every speck of the way all the way home. I *was* home.

I loved it that I could tell them that around the bend a certain landmark would turn up, bridge, church, old tractor up on a mound of dirt that the farmer had put up to mark his heritage for the traveler. It gave me much esteem in their young hearts.

And I heard many times from the back seat that old standard question: "How much further?"

They would ask mom first, and she would give them a general approximation: a hundred miles, fifty miles. That wasn't much fun, so they would ask me. I would make up some outlandish answer: "One hundred and eleven miles and three tenths."

My wife would give me the look, but on one occasion after one of my cute answers I saw that at least one of my boys was impressed. I heard Ryan say, as sotto voce as a kid can, to his brother: "Dad's smarter than mom. He's been to college." That opinion was obviously based on all the years of seeing me dash off to night college after supper and not on demonstration of knowledge.

Later, when they had learned of dad's true mental limitations, the question changed as did the order of the seat of knowledge. When the distance question would get an outlandish answer from me...*then* they would turn to mom and ask: "How much farther, mom? Really."

Now, there is no doubt in any mind in the universe, especially mine, that their mother was light years ahead of me in smarts. But she was also gracious.

LESSON 55

Make ice cream.

There is very little more pleasant in my memory than the sound of an ice cream maker churning away in the back yard. We would check it often waiting impatiently for it to be done. When we finally got to eat it was always so much better than store bought ice cream.

My ice cream is never as good as that in my memory, but I've tried to duplicate those summer evenings with the sound of an ice cream maker running in the back yard.

****

(Dad) Perhaps Ryan has lost his mother's homemade ice cream recipe, or my stellar technique at tending an old ice cream churn. I came from a long ancestry of ice cream churners.

In fact, for many years I used the man-powered, hand-crank ice cream makers — before the wonder of the electric motors. But the great thing about the hand crank ones: you could feel the ice cream making under your hand, gauge the thickening of it, and know exactly when it was ready to eat—and you burned off the calories making the ice cream that you would put on eating it.

We made ice cream often when our kids were coming up. No backyard party was complete without it. As Ryan said, there was magic in the sound of that ice cream maker whining away on the back patio as we played games. That whine was always accompanied by laughter. Families got together for every special holiday or any opportunity back then.

I still love homemade ice cream. There are no preservatives. It has to be eaten immediately—until it was all gone. Hey! You *have* to overeat. You can't waste good homemade ice cream, now can you?

What made the ice cream so good was the secret ingredient I used in churning it—joy. That and my wife's superb recipe.

LESSON 56

Leave projects unfinished.

Some things must get done, but many others can wait. You could have finished out the inside of the garage much earlier, but it went unfinished for years.

You could have taken the time you spent with your kids and wife and used it to finish many projects, but your priorities left many jobs unfinished.

****

(Dad) I made the garage water tight, completely finished outside, usable. That was a necessity; aesthetics could always wait. There were more important things.

Ordinarily I am a nitpicker, a neat freak, abhorring things left unfinished. But, through the years, I did leave so many jobs — like the garage — functional but incomplete. It looked good on the outside to the neighbors, at least.

But there is always so much left to do when raising a family. I did envy those folks who could afford to have a nice house built, garage all complete inside, sheet rocked, painted neat, shelves installed, yard in, landscaping done. I built my house in a nicer neighborhood than I could have afforded to hire someone else to build. We had a nice home as a result--before we could have afforded to pay for such a custom home to be built. It was all neat and finished on the outside, but inside were a few things needing finishing. But inside was a happy family.

A house is built from the outside in; a home...and a good character is built from the inside out. Raising kids should perhaps be that way too...you concentrate on the inside and don't get too picky with the outside. Always with kids a good inside will show up eventually in a good outside.

And it is especially true in raising up yourself. Don't worry about style, about what car you drive. We spend fortunes on cars, often more than we can afford--to impress someone else who won't care whether we live or die.

Yes...my first priority was wife and kids. I don't think it had to do with any great commendable sense of duty, or testament of great character in me. I just loved being with them.

LESSON 57

Buy the best for those you love.

Although you saved for retirement and spent little money on yourself, you have always been generous with your family. You bought us the best.

When I was getting married I asked you about how much I should spend on an engagement ring. You told me I'd never regret it if I bought the best that I could.

I've never regretted it.

****

(Dad) I have many regrets in my growing-up relationship with my family. So many times I kicked myself around the block for bonehead things I did. I blew it many, many times. But always it was not because of lack of love, but lack of wisdom. Also, failure frequently followed loss of temper.

A friend of mine from the military had an expression for someone who had done a stupid thing: "He's only got about ten brains." I took that as not being very smart. Apparently on that scale, about a million brains would be the minimum needed to be able to feed oneself.

For some of us, when we lose our tempers, we lose the precious few brains we had to begin with—losing down to just ten brains. I had to grow up too. I'm still having to learn new lessons. I'm still trying to find a few brains to augment my short supply.

But one thing I have learned absolutely: spending money on your wife is the best investment you'll ever make. And spending money on your kids, and others you love is your second-best investment.

Ryan Russell

LESSON 58

Put yourself in the way.

    I have a vivid memory of a dangerous dog approaching the house. We were out in the yard and small kids make easy prey. As the dog came at us, you grabbed whatever weapons were at hand, bricks in this case, and you got in between that dog and us. I can remember the dog and the fear I felt. I also remember the look on your face. The dog saw it too because it ran from you as you came at it.

****

    (Dad) Good for me. For once I did something right. I did good. But I'm afraid it was only instinct.
    We go crazy over some girl, and can't even begin to think of not having her exclusively always. We ask her to give up her freedom and come hang out with us, and only us, for the whole rest of her life. Then we have kids without even thinking about it because the little we did think about it was like, WOW! I want to have kids with this fantastic girl. And you're a goner: you end up loving those little ones as much as you do your wife, because they are a part of you and a part of this fabulous girl you get to live with, and all is right in the universe.

You do all that, not because you sat down and agonized over the wise decision to make. It was all instinct. And guess what? God planned it to be all that way. Because He knew we would never have many more than about ten brains with which to figure it out for ourselves.

And low and behold...if anything ever tries to lay a hand on what you love...those lives you love a million times more than your own...well, God help them. Instinct takes over again. You don't go off and plan a clever campaign to overthrow the villain. Not in the least. You just jump headlong between them and any threat to the most valuable things in your universe, and you lay everything you have on the line. And you never give one fraction of thought for your own self or your safety when you do.   Not one fraction.

LESSON 59

Write your kid's stories.

Several times in my life, I've had thoughts for stories. From a kid's half-formed idea to an adult's broken dream on a sleepless night, you listened to my ideas.

From apple trees, to an Irish immigrant, to a fractured moon, you've listened and turned them into wonderful stories. The ideas have faded, and the dreams have been forgotten, but the stories remain.

****

(Dad) As a writer I wish I had Ryan's imagination and vast store of thoughts worth telling. I have turned many of those thoughts into stories, and have a treasure trove of others with books already sketched out. They surpass the many ideas that have come from only my own small head.

The first grade in school turned him on to the written word. He wanted to write a story about Mary and the Apple Tree. It was a fine idea. He illustrated it, provided the plot and I touched up some of his writing.

Another early masterpiece was a poem and the illustration which was of only a lion. The poem:

> Here lies Ryan
> Who was eaten by a lion.

On one of his solo projects that same year he wrote a story of intrigue with a bit of humor. His protagonist in the end dispatched the dastardly villain with a gun. The clever line went thus:

"I knew I would have to shoot him with a forty-four. I did not have a forty-four, so I shot him twice with a twenty-two."

Ryan's "Irish immigrant" who faced sure death from a deadly outlaw as he tried to settle on a patch of land in the west, became "Outlaw." It has a clever twist.

The fractured moon story became "Moon Rocks." It is a futuristic, apocalyptic tale of future drilling for valuable minerals discovered on the moon by greed-driven industrialists. The drilling, in spite of warnings by the hero, touches off internal explosive elements deep in the moon's core that blow off huge hunks of the moon and send them on a destructive rendezvous with the earth.

You can read tales in my short stories book.

But the fun stories were Mary and the Apple Tree and others from the time when a little boy shared his imagination with his dad, and dad was thrilled to write them down.

LESSON 60

Make me smarter.

I don't mean "teach me more" or "sharpen my intellect."

I mean that you have always made me feel smarter than I am. You have a way of listening to my advice and immature "expertise" that truly makes me feel like an expert. You make me feel smarter than I really am.

****

(Dad) Ryan was always sharp, and I enjoyed hearing his ideas and philosophies. Still do. But me, on the other hand...I was a mere dumb farm kid, almost on the negative side in world-wise thinking--inferior at every age in comparison to Ryan. And I don't believe the fault was mere environment.

My dad was always busy. He had a large farm to run and farming then and now is the busiest of occupations—a thousand acres of cotton to be planted, cultivated, hoed, fertilized, fumigated, harvested, two or three hundred animals, mules, horses, cows, hogs, chickens. I could go on. Houses, barns, equipment. Many mouths to feed. Several families depended on my dad.

Farming back then--and sometimes even now--is a crap shoot business where you rolled the dice on the weather, too much or too little rain, and on the boll weevils, cut worms, locusts and a million others, on the laborers—would they die or walk off, would the mules get sick and die, when, not if—and those mechanical nightmares, wagons and such, and later tractors, cotton pickers and combines--would break down, usually when needed most—all of those variables. And finally, *if* you made a decent crop, and *if* the rain held up while you picked the cotton--that wasn't the end. Facing you then was the world commodities financial market. The market could drop at the most inconvenient time and wipe you out forever. In addition to that, my dad always ran a cotton gin during picking season, working the farm by day, and the gin half the night.

My dad taught me a lot about farming and hard work. He taught me as much safety as he could, especially one little safety tip—never lay a hand on any moving part of a cotton gin, especially a huge conveyor belt that snatched off his right thumb forever.

But dad had precious little time to just spend with me, our annual hunting trips being the exception.

My mother, on the other hand, took time with me. She had more time with me than dad, but only because her chores put her with me more often. She picked cotton right along with the rest of us during picking time.

And she was always so very interested in anything I might think up. She listened with a gleam in her eye and that always precious loving smile. And those dreams I thought up WERE the most interesting thing a human could possibly hear, at least my mother made me think so.

Ryan had a great mind. All my kids amazed me. (Thanks to their intelligent mother). I loved watching my kids go from the first small, cute ideas and kept watching as those ideas grew along with them in maturity and into very great and fascinating workings put into practice.

I am not the slightest bit concerned that my kids have long ago eclipsed the very best ideas I could ever come up with. Not at all.

I want them to be as great as my mother thought I could one day be.

LESSON 61

Work for your family.

You worked long hours when I was growing up. You didn't do it because you were a workaholic or just loved your job. You did it to take care of your family. To pay for the things we needed.

You took care of our home and family. I only hope the same can be said of me by my children.

****

(Dad) This one is easy. That is, the concept was easy. The need was there and I was blessed to have the health and opportunity to go make the money to supply the need—not all the wants—but the needs.

It did require my time, but the need for resources was greater than my leisure time. We weren't rich, but we were blessed. I was able to work long hours on my regular job, and for years worked weekends roofing houses—very hard, hot work.

Somehow, somewhere in me was the voice that spoke truth: a man should take care of his family. I listened. But it was my honor rather than a burden. My overall most satisfying accomplishment of my life was the taking good care of my family.

LESSON 62

Show me how to love.

All my life you showed me what love looks like. The way you loved mom. The way you loved us.

If I fail to love, the fault is mine alone. I can never claim ignorance of knowing what loves looks like in action.

****

(Dad) Ryan perhaps gives me more credit than due me, or gives me credit I don't deserve. I was taught, my own self, what love looks like—by my sweet and selfless mother who loved long, hard, relentless--come whatever. It was a sweet, quiet, always-giving love.

But in Ryan's time, while he was watching me, I was also in the process of learning what love is and looks like—from his mother, my wife—one of the most unselfish and loving people I have ever known.

LESSON 63

It's okay not to heal.

It's common wisdom that you will always heal. You will get over it eventually. But what happens when you don't?

The way you loved mom and the way you continue to even 15 years after her death has taught me much about the fallacy of healing. Life moves on, but sometimes you never heal, and that's okay.

****

(Dad) The common saying--Time Heals all Wounds--unfortunately is not true of all wounds. Time might close the wound with scars, but down inside the wound is fresh and paining, and will remain so until the grim reaper finally closes the wound.

I see it in many a mother's eye who has lost a child. She smiles, even laughs, seems to be full of joy—yet, even while she laughs she remembers the hurt. It is a numb pain that will never go away.

Some have said, don't make any decision for one year after losing a spouse. That's good advice — for during that year some of us can't think good enough to even remember to eat. For some, mercifully, a year will do it. They hold a vigil of honor for three hundred and sixty-five days, then shed the widow's weeds and take up life again.

But for some of us, three hundred and sixty-five days is not even the first inch of a million miles back to healing, to sanity and reason.

I am thankful to Ryan and my other kids for allowing me to continue to carry the torch. I tried to be upbeat for my kids, knowing their own hurt, but deep down beneath the scars, as it might ever be, is the unhealed wound.

LESSON 64

Always believe in those you love.

I know that I have given you plenty of reason not to, but you never stopped believing in me. There was a time when I no longer believed in myself or that my life would ever amount to anything, but your belief sustained me.

When I didn't believe in myself, you believed in me, and it was enough.

****

(Dad) A teenager usually thinks his dad is an out-of-touch old fogey whose time has passed and who has not the mental acumen to even have a clue of the modern culture. I know; I was a teenager. I was nuts for "You Ain't Nothin' But a Hound dog," and "Maizy Doats and Dozy Doats." Man, was I brilliant.

I was crazy about those songs and many other popular songs of my young years. But I know that my parents had their music and my kids theirs, and few of us understand the others.

It's a generational thing. It will always be thus. I tried to see my kid's love of their music as I did mine back then. I even like much of it.

Now…I don't fathom tattoos, and I sure don't get the sense in punching holes in your flesh and hanging something off it—especially eyebrows, tongues and other unmentionables. Yeah—maybe it's the old fogey coming out. But I did appreciate much of the music of my kid's era and beyond. Certainly not all.

As I said, it's generational. Every age has its themes, cultures, music—and naïve idea that their parents were dinosaurs. And I'm sure my kids were just like me as a kid, thinking the old ones are not hip—or whatever the kids call "cool" now—if "cool" is even a word they ever heard. But my kids had fun teasing me about my "antique music," and laughed as I lampooned theirs.

None of us comes here very smart. Else we would need no one to feed us and change our diapers. So, it is good for a parent not to get too upset when his fledgling tries his new, untested wings. Just be there with the net.

And parents, if they watch closely, will see the potential in their kids beyond the "I-know-everything" period. I saw potential so great in Ryan, that if he hadn't had a mother equally as smart, I might have thought we had a switched-at-birth scenario.

I knew back then that Ryan had all the tools necessary to accomplish anything in this world he wanted to accomplish. The trouble with teenagers and their perpetual confidence in their superior knowledge, is their equally perpetual uncertainty of how to employ it. They know they know, but the world sometimes looms dark and predatory to them.

Then it is the parents' job to fold them in love and let them know that their parents and God are with them, and with that team in their corner, coupled with their rock-solid punch of youth and sharp minds, they can step into the ring and knock down Rocky Marciano. (Now, to you kids…Rocky Marciano is…. Never mind.)

LESSON 65

Forgive.

Who has done you wrong that you have not forgiven? I can think of no one.

You once said that you wanted nothing to stop God from forgiving you and so you would forgive others.

Talking forgiveness is easy, but practicing it is not. And yet you have shown me what it means and what it looks like to forgive.

****

(Dad) Forgive me...for not being that perfect.

I guess, in my life, forgiveness is the hardest of all virtues to grab hold of and hang onto. You would think I would have it down pat by now. I've had many lessons.

Even recently I got a booster shot.

I was at a concert and was taking pictures with my cell phone. The man behind me tapped me on the shoulder and said rather smartly that he had come to see the show, not see me take pictures of the show. I got pretty steamed. Forgiveness evaporated from my vocabulary.

After the show, he tapped me on the shoulder again—this time he apologized and genuinely ask my forgiveness.

I learned two quick lessons: one, I had failed the forgiveness test. And two, he owed me no apology. He had been right. I was wrong. It had been rude of me to be blinding him with my cell phone during the concert.

Forgiveness is a hard one. I've flunked the exam so many times. Fortunately, God is patient. He gives me remedial training, and then springs the test on me once again. Perhaps one day I'll get a passing grade.

LESSON 66

Have faith in God.

Faith is easy when times are easy. Having faith in God when times are tough is not.

When mom died you taught me so much about how to fight for faith. I watched you work and wrestle for faith. I saw you agonize over questions without answers.

Through that devastation, you showed me how to have faith in God.

****

(Dad) And speaking of hard lessons....

When my wife of thirty-two years suddenly died—one second alive, holding my hand, then next second—dead, that great life gone, that bright light gone out, way too young--a thing happened to me that I could never imagine—I died mostly that day too. My life had been sucked out...I was numb...I was broken...a great earthquake had opened up and swallowed my heart and soul. If not for three equally as devastated pairs of questioning, needy, badly hurting eyes looking back at me, I wished to die myself. Life would never be worth much ever again. I cried--me, a man who never cried—I cried until I thought I could have filled up an ocean, and the tears were still endless.

The suddenness of it. It began as a happy day—December ninth, a Saturday. I had just worked my last day of the year, having saved all my vacation for Christmas time. Today, I had washed the cars and done the chores. Sunday was church, then Monday, my wife and I would hit the department stores to find treasures for our kids. But tomorrow would never come. One day--happiness, hope. We were finally pulling out of the financial struggle to put kids through college, finally seeing clear skies and smooth sailing—happiness; the next day, the next second—all life, all hope--gone.

Why had God been so cruel—after we had gone through the struggles and finally could see the joy ahead—why such an end of joy?

But the one thing I pledged to do was not blame God. It was life. Life was not guaranteed. But didn't God create life? Didn't he hold life? Couldn't He, at a thought change fate? I couldn't pray. No one was listening.

But I did struggle to refuse to think all those thoughts—to blame God for this black misery that had descended on all that I was. For those first few killing months I was successful. But months later, smug in my success, when I had let down my guard, the hard thoughts came. I needed someone to blame. I chose God. And I blamed myself. If I had only treated her right, as she so wonderfully deserved, God would have let me keep her. How many times have I gone through the litany of every time I let her down. I knew, and know well that I was not worthy of her. Why had I not totally put her up on that ivory pedestal that she was so worthy of and worshiped at her feet? Why was I such a fool?

I even let my kids down while I was in the dark ocean of despair, a sure regret.

I finally had to try to take hold of my life, my emotions and face everything that was to be--for my kids and grandkids. I was going to live, and since I was, I had to get on with it. Oh, I had been doing everything I was doing before, going to work, taking care of the house. My daughter who was still living at home-- nineteen. I tried to become both father and mother. We tried to have a home. We caught ourselves looking at each other.

But I had not begun to live again. I continued inwardly to grieve. I could smile and talk, but all the while I felt like I was trying to hold my guts within my body.

But I kept climbing, out of the deepest valley of my life—and ever reaching out a hand to me were my kids, ever faithful. And the hand of God was reaching too. He sent another good woman to help me.

What I have learned—faith is not quick, it is not instant. It takes some of the longest, hardest work of a lifetime. And it takes loving hands reaching out.

LESSON 67

Make your parents proud.

Papaw Russell didn't show his feelings often, but I saw that he had a deep respect for you.

Mamaw beamed when she looked at you. I know she loved all her kids, but the way she looked at you told me you were her favorite.

You made your parents proud.

****

(Dad) I don't know if I was my mother's favorite. She loved us all. But I was her baby boy, and for eight years, her baby. And she had the greatest capacity I have seen for love. Our bond was perpetual and unbreakable—not even by death, I have found out.

We had three good kids. Let me brag on my kids. Yours are fabulous, I can see. But mine are mine. And all of them have tender, loving hearts, and they always, all the time show tremendous love for their father.

My kids have their differences, naturally, but they also share family traits and looks. But mostly they share the greatness of the heart. To repeat a broken record: they got that from their mother. And that is no empty platitude from me.

And how very much they all make me proud. Each one of them are great people, great citizens, honest, trustworthy, hard working, God fearing. They hold themselves accountable for their actions.

Which of my kids is my favorite? Each and every precious one of them. They're great kids. And yes...they take after their mother.

All my kids have made their parents so VERY proud.

LESSON 68

Be gentle.

You never demeaned. You were never condescending. You never abused me. You never abused your authority.

You loved and led your family with a gentleness of spirit handed down to you from your mother. Hopefully some small measure of that gentleness will be found in me as well.

****

(Dad) Be assured that Grandma's loving kindness is alive and well in her grandchildren. Ryan loves his kids, leading them in that love, and never shows anything else to them. And they are good, loving kids. All three of my kids have that love and gentleness for their own children, thanks to their grandmother, thanks to their mother.

I never see a hardness in my kids as they raise their kids, even in discipline. But I see love abounding. The hand of discipline is wearing a feathered glove.

One thing I didn't want to do is tear my kids down with angry rebuke and criticism. I knew what a lasting impression it could make. Many kids in our day still bear the scars of severe discipline—not the visible scars of the club, but those hidden by the whip of criticism.

A whipped dog will always be whipped. He will cower until he is pushed to breaking, and then explode in viciousness. And it is so with people. We see it every day in our society.

I know grown people, middle aged even that have those mental scars from childhood which they try to hide beneath a smile or gruff exterior. A child mentally abused will never get over it. He will learn to reconcile the hurt, but can never completely forget it.

God help us parents to learn that.

LESSON 69

Love the Lord.

This lesson is so much more than a Sunday school lesson. It's about the measure of a person's faith over the course of a lifetime.

Now more than ever you show your kids that you have a deep love of Jesus Christ. You modeled this for us over your lifetime, even if you occasionally didn't pay close attention to a Sunday morning sermon and wrote poetry instead.

****

(Dad) I wrote several hundred poems in church, sometimes because the sermon became monotonous, and other times because it was inspiring and inspired in me a thought. I have compiled those poems into books which I have titled "Sunday Morning Poetry" — volumes one through eight and counting.

I don't apologize for my faith in God and in Jesus Christ.

I freely admit to a great love for my Lord Jesus Christ. To know him is to love him. Many have done good and great things for me, but none have ever given their lives for me.

So many say they don't believe in God. We weren't divinely created. There was this big bang in space and out came a Mount Rushmore. It also created a primordial swamp from which the monkey crawled out.

I'm sorry. It takes much more faith to believe in evolution than in creation. And who created the first matter from which things evolved and the time and space in which it existed. And is the sun still evolving? Will it get colder and turn us into ice cycles, or hotter and chicken fry us? Come on. Global Warming? Get real.

There is historical record for Jesus Christ. He lived and died a horrible death. But he lives yet. Those who welcome him have a peace and stability down in their inmost parts that nothing of the world can give — from the living Christ.

Be not deceived. Perhaps it's easier to believe in Satan. A world of chaos and misery is plainly evident in our present eyes. The record of the purveyor of that evil was first recorded at the dawn of time.

There are evil men in the world. They give no place to Jesus. But there are good men too, men who have peace here because they have invited into their hearts the lover of their souls and the guarantor of their eternal, peaceful homes that surely exists after this life.

You won't find peace in the god of this world, revel as you might. Peace in our lives comes only from the presence of the one who died for us living in our hearts.   Yes, I certainly do love Jesus.

LESSON 70

Give a boy more than 70 reasons.

Over the course of my life I have so much more than 70 reasons to love you. I have learned so much more than 70 lessons.

I am not expressive with my emotions, but I love you deeply and I am so grateful that you are my dad. You have given me much more than 70 reasons to be proud to be called your son.

****

(Dad) Oh how I wish I would have been that great man Ryan thinks I was.

I hope you did better than me, in your lives and relationships with your children. I hope you were the dad Ryan describes in his wonderful book. As Dickens also says: "If I could work my will...." But I would complete the thought this way: If I could work my will there would be peace on earth...and most especially between fathers and sons and of course, between all parents and their children.

Nothing in this world equals the wonderful blessings of peace and love in the home, especially between parents and their children. And nothing equals the misery of the absence of that peace.

Peace comes from love, from each other and from God.

I wasn't blessed with great intelligence. I made so many dumb mistakes.... But I was saved by the truth: love covers a multitude of sins. I was blessed with love—unnaturally great love for my kids. I can't say where it came from, maybe from the perfect example of it from my mother. But I would say it came in the greater part from God.

Don't ever even begin to put me up on the pedestal of saint. I am a sinner...saved by the grace of God. I was the Prodigal Son for whom God had to continually kill the fatted calf. But my great desire was to be a saint. I worked hard at it (most times) but I always failed. But God always opened his arms and received my apology with great love.

It was easy to be gentle with my children, to slave for their comforts, to fiercely protect them from all comers, so very easy…because I loved them so very much. I loved them far more than myself, with a celestial love that transcended my lousy human self. It was God's love for me passed on to them.

If you are a father, let me recommend your kids to you:

They are you, the best in you.

They are not yet perfect; they can become beautiful.

They are given to you--not for you to make them perfect--but to make them good, kind, loving grown people.

They stand ready and willing to give you all their love and all their honor.

They want to take great pride in you, to repay your goodness with being good honorable sons and daughters.

They want to love you.

And what they want from you, what they need more than any other thing upon the face of the earth, even if they might not know it, is your love.

Thank God for giving me that love for my kids. When I failed them I could almost hear them say:

"It's ok dad. Nobody's perfect. We know you love us. That's enough."

www.ingramcontent.com/pod-product-compliance
Lightning Source LLC
Chambersburg PA
CBHW052055070526
44584CB00017B/2185